Get the Degree Without Losing Your Mind

Get the Degree Without Lsing Your Mind

The Busy Student's Guide to Study Hacking

Christina Carmelle Lopez, MBA, MIA

NEW YORK

LONDON • NASHVILLE • MELBOURNE • VANCOUVER

Get the Degree Without Losing Your Mind

The Busy Student's Guide to Study Hacking

Published in New York, New York, by Morgan James Publishing. Morgan James is a trademark of Morgan James, LLC. www.MorganJamesPublishing.com

Proudly distributed by Publishers Group West®

A **FREE** ebook edition is available for you
or a friend with the purchase of this print book.

CLEARLY SIGN YOUR NAME ABOVE

Instructions to claim your free ebook edition:
1. Visit MorganJamesBOGO.com
2. Sign your name CLEARLY in the space above
3. Complete the form and submit a photo
   of this entire page
4. You or your friend can download the ebook
   to your preferred device

ISBN 9781636981963 paperback
ISBN 9781636981970 ebook
Library of Congress Control Number:
2023935888

Cover Design by:
Rodrigo Corral

Interior Design by:
Chris Treccani
www.3dogcreative.net

Interior Graphics Designed by:
Christopher Kirk
www.GFSstudio.com

Morgan James is a proud partner of Habitat for Humanity Peninsula
and Greater Williamsburg. Partners in building since 2006.

Get involved today! Visit: www.morgan-james-publishing.com/giving-back

• • • • • • • • • • • • • • • • •

*For my parents, who didn't have the opportunity to go to college,
yet never failed to sacrifice their time, money, and energy to
support and further my education. All that I am, or hope to be,
I owe to you. Mom and Dad, I'm forever in your debt.
Thank you.
I love you.*

• • • • • • • • • • • • • • • • •

"I am still learning."

~ Michelangelo (at age 87)

TABLE OF CONTENTS

· · · · · · · · ·

FOREWORD

· · · · · · · · · ·

I know Christie from our work together at Pepperdine, where I personally observed her executive management skills in action. Christie was an instrumental leader in our launching of a major strategic initiative for the university. So, if anyone knows how to instruct busy students on personal effectiveness, it's her. She is thoughtful, intentional, and efficient. Using the strategies she outlines in this excellent book, she skillfully managed multiple demands and produced a massive amount of exceptional work in a very short time—all while getting her MBA.

This book is more than simply a collection of study skills or "hacks"—though it has those too. *Get the Degree Without Losing Your Mind* challenges students to think about their education holistically and encourages them to nurture not only their minds, but also their bodies and spirits. The skills students learn in this book lay the foundation for immense academic, personal, and professional success.

As a professor, dean, and now President of Pepperdine University, I regularly encounter students who struggle to find balance amidst the pressures of higher education. Many of these students also have full or part-time jobs. Some are student athletes. Others have families. And today, as attention spans wane, students of all ages are more distracted than ever. The advice provided in this book acts as an antidote to the distracted mind by helping students improve their ability to focus.

While many of the time-saving techniques in this book have been traditionally marketed to executives, this book combines the best of the personal effectiveness and time-management genres and makes it accessible to students at all levels. Furthermore, *Get the Degree Without Losing Your Mind* not only offers practical study tips, but it also serves as a guide to managing competing priorities and finding career direction. In fact, you'll probably want to reference the career development chapter for many years to come.

After more than a quarter century of working with students in higher education, I can confidently say without hesitation or equivocation that learners of all ages and life stages can benefit from the wisdom in this book. In fact, I utilize many of the tips for personal effectiveness (such as list-making) myself.

Get the Degree Without Losing Your Mind is both insightful and informative, and I haven't seen anything else like it on the market. I'm delighted you've decided to improve your study skills, concentration, and personal effectiveness by reading this book.

Best wishes for your continued success,

Jim Gash
President and CEO of Pepperdine University
Malibu, California
April 2023

INTRODUCTION

· · · · · · · · ·

Education. Faith. Family.

Growing up as a "hyphenated" American, those values were my family's top priorities—typically in that order. As the first in my family to graduate from college (and later graduate school), I've never taken my education for granted, largely because of the sacrifices I watched my parents make throughout my life to support and further my learning journey. While education has been called the "great equalizer," sadly, we are still a long way from a society based on merit and blind to the many differences that divide us. What I can say with certainty, however, is that education opens doors. Knowledge creates the space for growth and opportunity, and when stewarded properly, it can be a powerful tool to further equity and justice in our communities and throughout the world. However, with knowledge comes responsibility, so it's with the preponderance of the gift of education I've been given that I share the contents of this book.

For me, higher education represents both the highest peaks and lowest valleys in my life. While achieving mastery and "flow" can be exhilarating, learning also requires immense vulnerability. Learning isn't always easy or enjoyable, but the feeling of accomplishing something difficult is well worth the inevitable lack of sleep and even the stress learning can bring.

This book is written to spare your sanity and help you achieve balance, perhaps even joy, throughout your academic journey. As a lifelong learner, higher education consultant, and former law school administrator, I'll be your guru—teaching you the hacks that will help you focus on what matters most, so you can supercharge your study time to create more space for other essential things in life like family, friends, career, and yes, even fun.

I've been both a full-time student and a fully-employed student, so I know firsthand that working while going to school is not for the faint of heart. Still, I'm here to tell you that you can do more than slog through your studies, living from coffee cup to coffee cup. Following the steps in this book will equip you with the tools to learn, work, live, and thrive.

Though I wrote this book with the fully-employed graduate student in mind, I believe the tips and tricks I share in the following pages can be helpful to *any* student in *any* course of study, particularly if you're pressed for time. (And what student isn't?) Undergraduates, student athletes, graduate students, and anyone who wants a balanced life while pursuing higher education can benefit from this book.

I want to warn you, however, that study hacking isn't about cutting corners. It's about making strategic choices that enable you to do more with less. In this book, I'll challenge you to work harder *and* smarter.

Learning isn't always easy, but it *is* worth it. You're investing in yourself and your future, so don't give up! Before you pick up your course textbook, heed the words attributed to Abraham Lincoln and first take a moment to "sharpen the ax" by reading this book cover to cover. You'll thank me later!

I wish you the very best on this journey.

Part I
The Busy Student's Guide
to
Study Hacking

CHAPTER 1

Know Your Why

*"What you do today can improve
all your tomorrows."*

~ RALPH MARSTON

The sun's rays were warm and unrelenting that spring morning as they bounced off the Pacific waters making its gentle ripples dance and sparkle like sapphires. After several years of working full time and taking graduate classes on nights and weekends, my triumph had finally arrived. As the seagulls swooped in the sky above, this surreal moment elicited joy—and deja vu. My name boomed from a nearby speaker as I stepped proudly across the outdoor stage, perched along the California coast, to receive my Master of Business Administration (MBA) diploma. But this wasn't the first time I'd experienced this moment.

I had lived this momentous occasion scores of times before. Whenever I was tired and tempted to give up, I walked across that stage. When I had to sacrifice leisurely activities for study sessions, I felt the weight and texture of the diploma in my hand and the corresponding joy in my heart. And eventually, what I envisioned for so long in my mind's eye, finally became

NOTES

a reality—and it can for you too. If you dream of getting a degree, or completing any course of study, but need practical advice and a little encouragement, allow me to be your guide, and let's dream big together.

Whether you're a busy undergraduate or graduate student, working or interning while in school, or a student athlete—this book is for you. Perhaps you're a mid-career professional taking evening or online classes. Or maybe you're an art or trade school student working full time and running a side hustle. If so, you're in the right place. It doesn't matter whether you're a traditional or nontraditional student. If you want more than simply to survive the next semester and desire to thrive in all you do, read on.

In this book, I'll teach you how to work smarter so you can achieve your goals and do more with less. The tips and frameworks I share here will prepare you for success in school and lay the foundation for personal and professional effectiveness. The advice in this book took a lifetime to learn, but I wrote it in a simple, straightforward manner because who has time to read *another* textbook? This book is about efficiency, so if you're ready to change your study habits and maybe even your life, let's get started.

Someone far wiser than me once said, "Begin with the end in mind."[1] So, before you do anything, I want you to ponder your reason for learning. Grab a pen. It's activity time!

Know Your Why

Exercise 1: What is your objective for this course of study?

First, take a moment to think about the big picture. Why are you pursuing this degree or course of study? Do you want a promotion or a new job? Do you want to make more money? Perhaps you simply wish to generate more options for yourself and maybe your family. Why is *completing* this degree or program important to you? Answering this question is an essential step in your success, so don't skip it. A time may come when you'll be tempted to quit, so you need to know your own intrinsic motivating force that will push you through to the end.

Assignment

Take a moment now and write down your "why."[2] Use the space below to record your answer. Then, I want you to close your eyes and visualize completing your goal: walking across a stage to receive your diploma, getting a promotion or that dream job, or whatever a successful finish looks like for you. What are the sights, sounds, smells, and tastes associated with this experience? How do you feel at this moment? Proud? Accomplished? Elated? Whatever the feeling, write it down.

EXERCISE 1: WHAT IS YOUR OBJECTIVE FOR THIS COURSE OF STUDY?

(A) Write down your "why."

(B) Visualize completing your goal. How do you feel? In as much detail as possible, write down what it looks and feels like to complete your goal.

Whenever you feel discouraged (and trust me, you will), I want you to come back to the "why" you wrote down, visualize the moment you achieve your goal, and feel all the great vibes that go along with it. Be sure you keep your "why" statement somewhere you can see it and access it regularly. A journal, bulletin board, or notes on your smartphone all work well.

Exercise 2: What is your objective for this specific class?

If you haven't enrolled in classes yet, you may need to return to this exercise. Likewise, I recommend you revisit this exercise every semester when you plan your coursework and study time for the semester. (More on this later.)

Assignment

Take a moment to consider the course or courses in which you're currently enrolled. Do you desire basic knowledge—or better yet, mastery—of one particular framework, concept, or tool? Or do you simply want to pass the class? Is your goal to get an *A* or a *C+*?

This question doesn't have a right or wrong answer, provided your response doesn't impede you from achieving your overarching objective from Exercise 1. Instead, your response will frame how you work and allocate time for this course. So, don't feel guilty about your answer to this question—just be prepared to own it.

For example, when I took Managerial Accounting during my MBA program, my only goal was to pass the course. Since I had no desire to become a CPA, I simply wanted to come away with a basic understanding of accounting principles and enough knowledge to analyze financial statements. That's it. I didn't need an *A* in the course, and I certainly wasn't going to be the teacher's pet. Making this agreement with myself saved me a lot of needless anxiety and stress. And when I felt overwhelmed, I asked myself one simple, clarifying question: "Is this (answer/problem/topic) truly something I need to know as a business owner, or is it something I can entrust to my accountant in the future?" That question helped me focus my energies on learning the mission-critical concepts for my personal success in the course and my goals as an entrepreneur. Your education is meant to serve YOU, your goals and objectives, so always remember to run your own race.

> *Your education is meant to serve YOU, your goals and objectives, so always remember to run your own race.*

Note that your answers to Exercise 2 will change from course to course and semester to semester. As you embark on this journey, you must become comfortable renegotiating your priorities regularly. Switching gears is okay if you remain focused on your "north star" (Exercise 1) and continue moving steadily in that direction, regardless of how fast or slow you go. So now it's your turn to be honest with yourself.

EXERCISE 2: WHAT IS YOUR OBJECTIVE FOR THIS CLASS?

Write down your personal objective for every course in which you are enrolled. Note that you may have multiple goals for a single course. For example, you might want to get an A in the course and achieve mastery of a specific framework.

Course Name	Personal Objective

Prioritizing Your Time

Not everything in life merits your attention, and far fewer things deserve your immediate attention. So when balancing a lot (work, school, family, friends), you need to make peace with priorities that shift from week to week. However, you also need to keep your long-term objectives at the forefront of your mind so you can adjust and pivot as needed without losing grasp of your ultimate goals. This is another reason you should keep your answer to Exercise 1, your "why," in a place where you can see it.

For instance, you'll want to prioritize your studies during and in the weeks leading up to midterms and finals. Perhaps this prioritization means waking up earlier to work on term papers or skipping happy hour for a week or two. If you're going on vacation, on the other hand, you may want to do all your reading and homework for that week ahead of time, so you can completely unplug and enjoy a much-needed break from your schoolwork while you recharge.

Planning Is Key

People often mistake "balance" for the interminable juggling act of "doing it all," or worse, a mindless game of *Whac-A-Mole,* extinguishing only the most urgent fires. On the contrary, achieving proper balance requires a thoughtful, strategic approach that involves renegotiating the "weight" or proportion of what you do daily and weekly. However, this process must be intentional—a result of careful planning and not simply how you feel in the moment. If you allow yourself to adjust priorities based on how you feel, you'll end up "prioritizing" the fun, easy activities over the more challenging tasks that help you achieve your long-term goals.

If you're not familiar with Stephen Covey's Management Matrix,[3] the following figure will help you understand the four quadrants of activities that compete for our attention on a daily basis. You may find, as I do, that the non-urgent but important activities in life tend to take a backseat to the many "urgent" but unimportant distractions vying for attention. Why do those Quadrant Four non-urgent / non-important activities, like scrolling social media feeds, distract us so? Well, largely because they're fun! But mindless entertainment doesn't necessarily serve your larger aims, as is true for most activities in this enjoyable but nonproductive quadrant.

Time Management Matrix

	URGENT	NOT URGENT
IMPORTANT	**Q1** Activities: • Crises • Deadline-driven projects • Pressing problems	**Q2** Activities: • Planning • Prevention • Recognizing new opportunities • Recreation • Relationship building
NOT IMPORTANT	**Q3** Activities: • Interruptions • Popular activities • Proximate pressing matters • Some calls, some mail • Some meetings, some reports	**Q4** Activities: • Busywork • Pleasant activites • Most social media • Some phone calls, some mail • Time wasters, trivia

Adapted from The 7 Habits of Highly Effective People
by Stephen R. Covey

As humans who enjoy passive entertainment, we'll always be tempted by the non-urgent and unimportant distractions in life, so rather than simply trying to ignore them, let's find a way to manage our impulses. I like to refer to the principle of prioritization as "eating your vegetables." And let's be honest, no one *really* likes eating their vegetables (unless they're smothered in saturated fat), even though we know they're good for us. And we especially don't want to eat our veggies after having a taste of dessert.

Do Difficult Tasks First

For this reason, I want you to commit to doing the most difficult thing first. In other words, I'm asking you to eat your vegetables before you even look at anything else on your plate.

Research shows people only have a limited amount of willpower on a given day.[4] With all the choices, decisions, interactions, and issues you deal with daily, if you start with the easy things, you'll never have the willpower to do the tough tasks later, unless you've created a habit. Research also suggests that activities require far less willpower once they've become habits, which is why I'm such a believer in planning. Planning enables you to respond to changes in your environment and subsequent shifts in priorities without losing grasp of your ultimate goal.

> *Planning enables you to respond to changes in your environment and subsequent shifts in priorities without losing grasp of your ultimate goal.*

Let me give you a real-life example. During my graduate program, I made a plan to study on Sundays and the night before each class. And I committed to follow that plan no matter what. For example, if I had a class on Tuesday night, I'd do all my readings and begin my weekly assignments for the course on Sunday. On Monday after work, I'd complete any remaining homework and review it before submitting the assignment the following day. This practice created a *system* that accomplished several things.

1. **I created a steadfast habit.**
   By dedicating Sundays and Mondays to schoolwork, I blocked off that time mentally and physically (on my calendar), which meant I didn't schedule other events on those days because I knew they were allocated for my studies. Once it was a habit, I didn't even have to think about it. I didn't have to convince myself to crack open the textbook on Sunday morning or Monday night; it was automatic. By not engaging in an internal tug-of-war, I saved energy and willpower for other things.

2. **Second, because I wasn't waiting until the last minute to complete my weekly assignments, I had enough time to get help if I encountered issues.**
   If I had a question about an assignment at 11:55 p.m. on Monday night, and my homework was due at 8 a.m. the next morning, I probably wouldn't get the help I needed in time, and my grade would suffer. A time cushion before deadlines is almost always an effective planning strategy.

3. **Finally, not only did working in advance prevent last-minute crises, but it also gave my brain time to absorb the material before I put it into action.**
   For that reason, I liked to do weekly readings first, ideally a couple of days before tackling the related assignment. That way, I had a day or two to let my subconscious ponder the problem before diving in. Did you know your brain organizes information while you snooze?[5] That's why "sleeping on it" is never a bad idea when you're learning something new.

A Note on Chronotypes: Larks, Night Owls, and Third Birds

People work best at different hours of the day, depending on their chronotype.[6] (Hint: If you call yourself a "morning person" or a "night owl," you probably know your chronotype.) While knowing when you work best is helpful, unfortunately, because of typical work and class schedules, we don't always get the luxury of choosing when we'll do our work. So, my best advice for you is the following.

First, if you're an early-morning person, also known as a "lark," you may want to consider waking an hour early to do class readings or homework. If you're a "third bird" (more of a mid- to late-morning person), you might consider using your lunch break to catch up on reading. If you're a night owl, you probably have it made in the shade (pun intended). The working professional or full-time student schedule is perfect for you since you hit your stride after dinner when the rest of the world is winding down.

Second, save those less mentally tasking activities for when your energy is the lowest. If you've made a habit of doing the hardest thing first, then what's left on your to-do list at the end of the day should be easy to accomplish with little energy. For me, my energy is the lowest right before bedtime. So, for example, if I know I can't read another word in a textbook without nodding off, I might switch to watching educational YouTube videos, listening to an audiobook, or folding laundry (better yet, listening to an audiobook *while* folding laundry).

Whatever your chronotype, do your best to use it to your advantage! If you can't study during your ideal time, remember what you just learned and turn your study time into a habit, so it becomes automatic.

CHAPTER 2

Planning Is Everything

"Plan your work, and work your plan."
~ NAPOLEON HILL

Congratulations! If you're preparing for the upcoming academic term, that means you've been admitted to a degree program or other course of study, and you should be proud of yourself. You've probably enrolled in classes and have a few weeks before the start of the new semester. Let's talk about what to do during that time to ensure your highest possibility of success.

How to Plan for the Semester

As soon as you register for courses, take a moment to block off every single class time for the semester in your calendar. Whether your calendar is digital or analog, ensure every class session through your final exams is recorded and visible when you're planning and scheduling other activities during the semester.

Then, block off the dates you intend to study and prepare for each class. I gave you an example of my study schedule in Chapter 1, but that's not the only option. You could plan to do all your class preparation over the weekends and leave the week free for work and extracurricular activities. Maybe you'd rather study for a couple of hours each weekday, either before or after work or class. Or, you could do what I did and dedicate one day on the weekend to studying and one night a week per class.

Whatever the case, keep the following academic ratio in mind. Generally speaking, most graduate-level courses (and even some undergrad courses) require twice as many hours of homework as class time each week. So, if you have one 4-hour class, you should probably plan eight hours for reading and homework during a typical week. If you're taking two or more courses, you'll need to allocate 16 hours, or more, to your studies. If it seems like a lot of time, that's because it is! One of the biggest mistakes I see students make is not allocating enough time for their coursework. While this book will help you utilize your study time more effectively, you also need to be realistic about the extent of the commitment you make when you choose to pursue an academic degree. You need to put in sufficient *quality* study time regularly to truly reap the benefits of higher education.

PLANNING ACTIVITY 1: ACADEMIC SEMESTER

☐ Mark all class times for the semester in your calendar so you won't inadvertently schedule something else during that time.

☐ Block off all the days and times you intend to study for each course.

It's perfectly okay to swap study days if something important comes up, but at least when you add that special event to your calendar, you'll see your prior academic commitment. That way, you can (and should) immediately reschedule your study time for that week.

How to Plan for a New Course

1. **Skim the syllabus.**

   Once you register for classes, you'll likely receive access to some course materials, including the course syllabus. Don't wait until five minutes before your first class session to read the syllabus! As soon as you can access it, download or print the course syllabus and review it. This document will tell you some valuable things you need to know to prepare, such as:

   - What textbooks/materials to order
   - Whether or not an assignment is due on the first day (Surprise! Most graduate-level courses require some reading or homework before the first day of class, so be prepared.)
   - How much homework and reading the course entails (This is important when scheduling weekly study time for each course.)
   - Whether or not the class requires a midterm and a final exam
   - Whether and when any research papers are due
   - What the highest-value assignments or exams are in the course (more on this later)

2. **Calendar your study time and any important exams or projects in advance.**

   You've already added class sessions and homework study blocks to your calendar. Now, it's time to get specific. I want you to calendar every major exam, paper, or project—and don't just log the due date. Remember to also add reminders leading up to the final deadline. Then, schedule specific times (in addition to your regular homework blocks) to work on these more significant assignments.

For example, if I know I have a research paper due, in addition to working on it during my regular study sessions, I'll also block off specific times dedicated solely to preparing for that assignment. I won't wait until a few days before the deadline to get started because I know my brain needs time to thoroughly absorb and work through the material to reach the highest levels of learning. (Refer to Bloom's Taxonomy in the Appendix for a visual guide to this process.) For most students, moving from the simplest levels of learning (rote recall) to being able to put new ideas into practice through application takes time. Mastering the complexity of analysis and generating new ideas based on the original material typically takes even more time. My guess is this process takes time for you too.

So, give your brain the time it needs to absorb new ideas fully. I guarantee the sooner you start thinking about and preparing for those term papers and exams, the better you'll perform in the end.

Assignment

Take a moment now to complete Planning Activity 2 below.

PLANNING ACTIVITY 2: ACADEMIC COURSE
☐ Enter the due dates of important exams, papers, or projects into your calendar.
☐ Set a reminder 1–2 weeks before these assignments are due (depending on their scope).
☐ Set a second reminder 1–2 days before their final deadline.
☐ Block off the days and times you intend to work on each project or study for each exam.

Going through the above process in each course will ensure that no major projects or exams sneak up on you. Trust me; you don't want to skip this step! It will ensure you have ample time to study and prepare, which, based on my experience, is the difference between "*A*" work and everything else. Time allows concepts to percolate and gives you the chance to revise and refine your work.

How to Read a Syllabus

1. Find Course Materials

The first thing you'll want to do when reviewing the syllabus is order any needed textbooks or materials. Shipping can take time, and some texts may be difficult to find or out of stock by the time the course starts, so get ahead by placing your order ASAP. This way, you'll be prepared for the first class session, especially if you have any assigned readings due that day.

2. Identify High-Value Activities

Second, look for the highest-value activities. In business, we use this concept to help organizations hone in on the products, services, or operations that have the most significant impact on their bottom line, and the same principle applies to you and your success in this course. As you review the syllabus, refer to your response to Exercise 2 from Chapter 1 (your personal course objectives). Identify ideas or activities in the syllabus that are most valuable to *you* based on your interest level, future career goals, etc. Now, highlight the assignments or exams that impact your grade the most. If your objective from Exercise 2 was to get an *A* in the class, then this information will be critical.

3. Note Group Work

Last, look for any team projects and highlight them as well. While group projects may not comprise a large percentage of your grade, they're still a priority because your work will impact others, and you never want to be the weakest link on a team project. You want to be the MVP! If you offer your team your best and earn a reputation as someone others can rely on, you'll train yourself for success both in and outside the classroom.

PLANNING ACTIVITY 3: SYLLABUS CHECKLIST

☐ Order textbooks and other materials.

☐ Look for any assignments due before the first class meeting.

☐ Highlight "high-value" activities:

- High percentage of overall grade
- Assignments/concepts that interest you
- Group projects

☐ Input important deadlines and exam dates in your calendar.

☐ Schedule dedicated time for exams, papers, and projects (in addition to your weekly study time).

CHAPTER 3

Timeout!

"For every disciplined effort there
is a multiple reward."

~ JIM ROHN

Can we pause for a moment, so I can tell you what a great job you're doing? If you've completed the activities and exercises in the preceding chapters and the semester hasn't even started, you're WAY ahead of the game. I hope you're proud of everything you've done so far to set yourself up for success.

Now, give yourself some positive self-talk or a special treat because here's the deal. According to James Clear, author of the bestselling book *Atomic Habits*,[7] you can use rewards to train yourself to do difficult things. So when times get tough, use this trick to motivate and inspire yourself. Now go find that carrot and take a bite! You deserve it.

Bonus Activity:

Use the formula below to create a positive study habit loop.

Start with the positive habit you want to create—for example, reading for an hour before bed. Then think of an appropriate and immediate reward upon completion. Maybe you'll light a candle, write in your journal, or listen to your favorite podcast. Knowing you have a desired activity to look forward to will inspire you to complete the more challenging and focus-oriented tasks. Over time, you'll create a positive feedback loop, and before you know it, your brain will associate reading with an enjoyable pastime.

Take a moment to create at least one positive habit loop below.

Habit Building Formula

Triggering Action (Desired Action) = Immediate Results (Desired Reward)

When I complete...	Then I will...
two chapters of reading	*watch an episode of my favorite show*
(desired action)	(desired reward)
When I complete...	Then I will...
(desired action)	(desired reward)

CHAPTER 4

How to Eat an Elephant

"The secret of getting ahead
is getting started."

~ MARK TWAIN

A s a young and aspiring concert pianist, I often hit roadblocks when learning new music—and not just any piece, specifically Bach Preludes and Fugues. These masterpieces had more notes in a single measure of music than I was used to playing in a whole song. To top it off, they were relentlessly fast, requiring perfect synchronicity between the right and left hands. In other words, if I skipped a beat, I was toast. Consequently, I'd let the kitchen timer that measured my minutes at the piano tick away while I sat paralyzed by the notes on the page. Because I couldn't play the whole melody, I chose not to play anything at all. Finally, after weeks of zero progress, my sage piano professor taught me a lesson I will never forget.

"How do you eat an elephant?" she queried rhetorically.

NOTES

21

The answer, in case you're wondering, is, "One bite at a time."

My guru then broke down the four-page monstrosity into sets of two manageable measures each. She bracketed them with a pencil. "Only work on these two measures for the next week," she said. "Play them again and again, and don't even look at anything else."

At that moment, something inside me shifted. The impossible became not only possible but well within reach. The elephant on my chest (pun intended) was lifted. Based on my teacher's proposed schedule, I mastered Bach's Prelude and Fugue in two short months—nearly the same amount of time I'd spent staring hopelessly at the notes on the page.

You may not be an aspiring pianist, but we all have daunting tasks that are so big we're afraid to start. My advice to you, particularly as you embark on a season of research papers and what seems like an endless amount of reading, is to break the impossible project into bite-sized tasks, and keep eating the elephant one bite at a time!

Projects, Tasks, and Subtasks

Now, let me show you how to turn big projects into manageable tasks. Let's start with something familiar: sending holiday cards. Sounds easy enough, right? We'll begin by thinking about all the tasks associated with the project, in no particular order.

First, you probably need to buy Christmas cards if you don't have some already. But what happens when you get to the stationery store, and you realize you don't know how many you need because you never made a distribution list? I guess you need to make a list first. When you do that, it dawns on you that you don't have current addresses for everyone on your list, so you'll need to reach out to get those and perhaps even wait for a response. When you eventually have your cards and your updated mailing list, you remember that you need stamps, which may mean you have to go to the post office during business hours to buy them so you can finally send your holiday cards.

Let's say you started the above process at the beginning of December. By the time you have all your materials, including updated addresses, and you've written your cards, it's already December 20th, and now you're standing in a long line at the post office with a stack of envelopes in hand, wondering if your cards will arrive before the holiday. Isn't there a better way to plan projects? Indeed there is.

Let's try this exercise again, this time with a project-planning mindset. Now that you've pinpointed all the *tasks* associated with your *project*, you'll list them in sequential order, which means your holiday card task list will look something like this:

PROJECT: SEND HOLIDAY CARDS
DEADLINE: DEC. 5TH
☐ Make holiday card distribution list.
☐ Confirm recipient addresses.
☐ Buy cards and stamps.
☐ Address and personalize cards.
☐ Mail cards before December 5th.

Notice again that each item is now listed in sequential order, with each task dependent on the preceding one. This step is vital because projects stall far too often due to things we didn't think of or realize we needed to complete. Thinking through the process from start to finish before you begin helps you plan accordingly and allows you to create an appropriate timeline. Once you know your deadline and have organized your tasks, you can easily attach a due date to each chore to stay on track.

Below is an example of what that might look like:

HOLIDAY CARD PROJECT TIMELINE	
Nov. 1	Draft distribution list and request updated addresses.
Nov. 7	Confirm receipt of addresses and follow up as needed.
Nov. 15	Buy holiday cards and stamps.
Nov. 27–31	Address and personalize cards.
Dec. 1	Send cards by mail.

After preparing the above schedule, I realize why I rarely send holiday cards—I tend to start the process too late! I usually don't even start thinking about sending Christmas cards until the beginning of December, when I realize I don't have the addresses or the supplies I need. Typically, the holiday rush pushes festive correspondence to the bottom of my list, and sadly this project doesn't get done.

Has the same thing ever happened to you? You can avoid this pitfall by planning large projects in advance and allocating specific time blocks to accomplish them. Here's what to remember most when project planning.

HOW TO PLAN A PROJECT
1. Break projects into tasks. 2. Break tasks into subtasks. 3. Once you've identified tasks and subtasks, organize them sequentially. 4. Then create a project timeline.

The larger the project, the more complex it will be. Unlike the Christmas card example, you'll also have subtasks associated with each task. So now, let's look at a more complex scholastic project and observe how to apply the principles we just learned to the academic "elephants" in our lives.

An Elephant Example

Let's say you're enrolled in a 10-week course with a 10-page paper due at the end of the semester. Following is an example of how to segment a significant project into bite-size pieces. (While you'll read a complete guide to writing research papers in the next section of this book, the example below is focused specifically on project planning.)

Note: This example is for illustrative purposes only. Individual project requirements will determine how best to plan.

EXAMPLE PROJECT: 10-PAGE RESEARCH PAPER	
Week 1	Review assignment guidelines. Look for grading criteria and highest-value components. Ask any general questions about the assignment.
Week 2	Begin cursory research. Surf the web for related topics. Go down rabbit holes if you need to, but find a topic that interests you.
Week 3	Determine your topic and find quality source material. Research scholarly articles and other primary sources. Start reading and taking notes.

NOTES

Week 4	Conduct more research and take notes.
Week 5	Develop thesis and draft preliminary outline. You'll want to review your notes before this step.
Week 6	Start writing. Draft 5-6 pages. Don't worry about perfection. Just get words on the page based on the outline and notes you drafted.
Week 7	Writing and revising. Draft 5-6 more pages. Revise the pages you wrote in Week 6.
Week 8	Edit and revise. Revise the pages you wrote in Week 7. Then, read the entire draft. Re-work outline as needed. Read the whole paper again and revise as needed.

Tip: Now is the time to perfect your paper's structure and flow. Don't be afraid to cut things out that don't fit. It's also a great time to go back to the assignment requirements to ensure you didn't miss anything. |
| **Week 9** | Add finishing touches. Write (or rework) your introduction and conclusion. Now, edit the entire paper for accuracy and clarity. Think about style, sentence structure, grammar, spelling, and overall flow. Add transitions. |
| **Week 10** | Cite your work. Add in-text citations (if still needed), Works Cited, and References pages. Review and finalize any appendix material.

Re-read the paper from start to finish multiple times, looking for different types of errors. For example, read once for style, once for tone, once for citations, and once aloud. Finally, run the paper through Grammarly (or another online tool or app) to catch any spelling or grammatical errors you missed. |

Below is another example of how you might want to organize your time. Note that I suggest drafting more than the required number of pages in both models. Why? Because during your editing process, as you combine and condense your thoughts, your page count will inevitably shrink. Similarly, as you revise your work and refine your sentence structure, your word count should also decrease. So, by planning for the editing process, you'll end up with 10 high-quality, substantive pages rather than 8 pages of research you're trying to stretch out with wordy sentences, wide margins, and larger-than-normal font.

Figure 4.1: Research Paper 10-Week Plan

Now compare the above schedules to what I see most students do: ignore the metaphorical elephant for two months and then go into "panic mode" in Weeks 9 and 10. In contrast, if you follow a timeline similar to the ones I proposed, you'll be kicking your feet up and sipping a glass of wine (if you're of age) the night before your deadline, while your fellow students, those who didn't read this book, are pulling an all-nighter. Cheers to you!

Project Planning Exercise

Assignment

Now it's your turn to practice. Think of a project. It can be personal, professional, or academic. Use the space below to complete the following steps.

1. First, write the project's name and deadline.
2. List all associated tasks and subtasks in the space below.
3. Number them in sequential order.
4. List each activity (one per row) from start to finish in the "Task/Subtask" column under "Project Timeline."
5. Develop your project due dates by starting with the final deadline and working backward.

When you complete this process, you'll have a workable project plan and timeline. You can apply this process to any major project, whether at school, work, or home. With these project planning skills, you'll be unstoppable!

Project Planning Worksheet

Project Title:	
Deadline:	

Tasks:

Project Timeline

Due Date	Task / Subtask
	Final Deadline - Project Complete

CHAPTER 5

Read Like a Rock Star

"The more that you read,
the more things you will know.
The more that you learn,
the more places you'll go."

~ DR. SEUSS

T he tips you'll learn in this chapter will transform your study time like nothing else. They have the power to take your reading from aimless and elongated to laser-focused and effective, and the best part is that you can begin practicing these tips right now while reading this book.

A Note About Speed Reading

I took my first speed-reading course at age 16 to help me prepare for college entrance exams. And while I found some of the techniques effective, I also discovered my comprehension was much lower when speed reading, which is okay if I'm reading a novel but not great if I'm trying to grasp complex ideas for the first time. There is one speed-reading tip, however, that I find particularly helpful. Using a guide—such as three fingers on my right hand, a bookmark, or even a note card—

NOTES

to focus and propel my eyes forward prevents my gaze from darting around the page and keeps my mind from wandering too. I'll leave it to you to research and experiment with speed-reading techniques if you're interested, but now let me share a method I think works even better for academic reading.

How to Supercharge Academic Reading

As a full-time graduate student in my early twenties, I read every word of every article (sometimes twice), took copious notes, and outlined textbook chapters with alacrity. But later in life, as a working graduate student, I didn't have that kind of time. I needed to find a way to supercharge my reading so the time I spent perusing would be highly effective and extremely efficient. Below is my foolproof method, which not only helps you read faster, but also boosts comprehension.

Supercharged (Pre)reading Method

1. ***Start by giving yourself a time limit.*** Projects have a way of expanding to the time we allow for them. For example, if you give yourself four hours to read your homework, your mind will wander, you'll break for coffee and snacks, and you'll likely waste a lot of time before getting to business. If you give yourself one or two hours to read, however, you'll be forced to focus and meet your deadline.

2. ***Next, read the introduction and conclusion sections before reading the entire chapter or article.*** Remember in the last chapter when I gave you a template for writing research papers and told you to wait until the very end to write the intro and conclusion? I recommend that approach because I want you to include only the most important, relevant, thesis-bolstering ideas in those two places, and you won't

have the clarity and subject-matter knowledge to write the introduction and conclusion until the body of the paper is thoroughly fleshed out. The same concept is true for most textbooks and academic articles: You'll find the main idea, or thesis, in the introduction and the "punchline," or most important conclusions, summed up at the end. So when you're reading, take advantage of learning the key takeaways *before* diving into the chapter or article, and you'll prime your mind for maximum comprehension.

3. ***Now, review every visual aid, graph, and figure, starting at the beginning.*** These items can be charts, tables, diagrams, etc. Think of visual aids as neon-lit signs directing you to something you don't want to miss. And remember, the author deemed this information so vital she said it twice—once in the body of the text and again visually. I find that if I can make sense of the tables and charts *before* reading the text, I'm already well on my way to understanding the core concepts.

Note: Because ideas tend to build on each other, always start from the beginning of the chapter or article when executing this step and the subsequent ones listed below.

4. ***Next, read all bold (or italicized) words and their definitions.*** Highlight any that stand out to you. Put question marks by terms that confuse you and return to them later.

5. ***Now, skim the sidebars.*** You can choose which ones to read in full, but at the very least, get a sense of their overall subject matter. Sidebars are particularly helpful in illustrating or illuminating theoretical concepts with real-life cases or examples. An anecdote from a sidebar

will often stay with me for years or even decades after I've forgotten the remainder of the text. Remember that stories stick, so use that to your advantage.

6. ***Finally, go back to the beginning and read every topic sentence*** (i.e., the first sentence of each paragraph). In my opinion, this step is the fastest, most efficient way to gather critical concepts in a concise format. Take a moment to consider the author's writing structure. When composing paragraphs, thoughtful academics often communicate the most important idea in the first sentence and then unravel it in subsequent sentences with more detailed supporting material.

Notice how I've done something similar in the above paragraphs? I share the main point first, and then I expand on it. I recommend you use this structure as well, especially when writing essays and term papers. (More on this in Part II.)

TIMEOUT

Let's pretend you just worked through the six previous steps using a textbook chapter. If I confiscated your reading material right now and asked you to tell me about it, could you? What if I asked you to write a summary paragraph of the main ideas? Could you do it without reading the entire chapter or article? My guess is you could. I'd also bet that after going through the pre-reading methodology—before even reading the complete text—you'd know a lot more than you think.

Try this exercise to test your comprehension after completing the pre-reading process. The key to supercharging your reading is to be *active*, and the six pre-reading steps force your brain to get curious and to

NOTES

try to fill in the gaps on its own. They take you from a passive bystander, watching the words on the page go by, to an active participant. So read standing up if you have to! Make notes in the margins. Write down questions you have as they come up. And highlight anything that stands out. Get engaged with your reading, and I guarantee you'll retain more.

Now, back to the Rock Star Reading Method.

7. **Last, read the full text.** Now that you know the most important ideas (bold words and their definitions, tables, figures, topic sentences, etc.), your brain is ready to focus on those concepts as you read. If you follow the steps outlined in the table below, you'll find yourself reading faster and remembering more of what you read.

ROCK STAR READING CHECKLIST FOR STUDENTS (FOLLOW IN ORDER)
1. Give yourself a time limit.
2. Read the introduction and conclusion.
3. Review all visual aids: charts, graphs, tables, and figures.
4. Read any bold words and their definitions.
5. Skim the sidebars.
6. Read every topic sentence.
7. Now read the full chapter or article.

Bonus Step 8: Notetaking

Next-Level Reading = Writing

If you've employed the active reading techniques you've learned so far, you probably have a textbook or academic article filled with (digital or analog) dog-eared pages, highlights, and notes. Your challenge now is synthesizing these scribbles into an organized and concise outline.

I know it sounds like a lot of work, but I'll tell you a little secret. Before, during, and even after graduate school, I would not only take notes on every book I read for fun, but I would also transcribe those notes from the book into a comprehensive digital document. This way, I had access to all my book notes in one place in case I wanted to review anything later. Sometimes my notes would be nothing more than bullet points denominated by chapter. Other times, depending on the nature of the book, I'd create detailed hierarchical outlines. I don't do this anymore (thankfully). However, I'm convinced this practice helped me hone the critical thinking skills required not only as a graduate student and a professional—but especially as a writer.

So here's the practice I suggest to move your reading skills into next-level comprehension. Once you've read a chapter in your textbook, I want you to commit to taking a few extra minutes to transfer your notes, highlights, etc., into a single document. You should add notes for each chapter weekly when you complete your assigned reading, and the information is still fresh. And by the time you get to the end of the semester, you know what you'll have? Not just a comprehensive outline of the entire text, but the perfect study guide for the final exam. (Can I get a mic drop, please?)

No Shame in the Audiobook Game

I used to be against audiobooks (except for light non-fiction) because I thought my brain processed words on a page more analytically than spoken words. Because I'm a visual and kinesthetic (versus auditory) learner, for me, that's probably true. However, once I started my MBA as a fully-employed graduate student, I saw audiobooks for what they truly are—a godsend!

My recommendation for any student is this: Always order the hard copy or electronic version of a text, but check to see if an audio version is also available. If you're short on time, you might only be able to listen to the audio version, but if you come across a concept or section you want to review again, having a hard copy is indispensable. (It also comes in handy for citations.) If you're a visual or kinesthetic learner, you'll probably still want to mark up and highlight the text even if you also listen. If you're really interested in a topic, you might even want to "binge" listening to the entire text, just to get ahead. And you can always review your paper or electronic version before each class session if you need a refresher on the material. As a life-long learner and voracious reader, I find that receiving information in multiple formats can help reinforce it.

Think of technology as your ally, and don't be too proud to use it when it's available. In addition to audiobooks, check out other apps and tools with text-to-speech technology. They can be helpful timesavers, especially during long commutes.

A Note on Learning Styles

Peter Drucker says, "Successful careers are not planned. They develop when people are prepared for opportunities because they know their strengths, their method of work, and their values."[8] According to Drucker, people learn by listening and reading (auditory versus visual learning) as well as writing, doing, and speaking (kinesthetic). You can read more about learning styles below.

AUDITORY LEARNERS

- Learn best through oral instruction
- Enjoy listening and also hearing themselves talk
- Prefer to hear or recite information and benefit from auditory repetition

Challenges: They can be easily distracted, especially by sounds. May have difficulty following written instructions.

KINESTHETIC LEARNERS

- Prefer to learn by doing rather than reading
- Like to participate in learning through hands-on activities

Challenges: Difficulty listening. May not enjoy reading. May find it difficult to pay attention to auditory or visual presentations.

VISUAL LEARNERS

- Learn best by reading or watching videos
- Typically like to read and take notes
- Remember by seeing words presented visually and viewing charts, maps, pictures, outlines, and diagrams

Challenges: Can be distracted by visual disorder or movement. Mind may wander during lectures.

To find out your learning style, take this brief quiz below. As a bonus, you'll learn your Myer's Briggs Personality Type (MBTI) too. I've taken a number of personal inventories, and I find this one to be both accurate and informative.

Assignment

Take the online quiz, then record your findings below.

LEARNING STYLE QUIZ

Want to know your learning style? Take a free quiz at learningstylequiz.com.

My Learning Style(s):

Key Takeaways from Quiz Results:

CHAPTER 6

Making Minutes Matter

"The bad news is time flies.
The good news is you're the pilot."
~ MICHAEL ALTSHULER

Despite the best preparation and planning, sometimes life catches us by surprise. When that happens—and it will—this chapter will help you manage your minimized time, even if all you have is an hour.

Focus Fuels Learning and Excellence

To make the most of every minute, you need to hone your ability to focus. According to Daniel Goleman, author of *Focus: The Hidden Driver of Excellence*, "We learn best with focused attention. As we focus on what we are learning, the brain maps that information on what we already know, making new neural connections."[9] If our minds wander, however, that new information is lost.

The following tips will help you eliminate distractions, find hidden time, and organize that time so you can focus better and increase the likelihood of achieving "flow," that Zen-like state of complete mental immersion.[10]

Tips for Achieving Focus and Flow

Tip 1: Turn it Off

Turn everything off, including your cell phone, television, and any background noise or music. Heck, turn off the internet if it distracts you! (If you can't go into "airplane mode," then use an application like Freedom to block access to specific websites, social media streams, and even the internet.) If you want to go Wi-Fi free and don't have a hard copy of the text, download your materials for offline reading or print them out ahead of time.

Note: I prefer hard copies to electronic versions whenever possible for several reasons. Not only do my eyes fatigue faster when I read online, but they tend to wander a lot more because I can't use the speed-reading technique I discussed earlier that works so well on the printed page. I also enjoy carrying a hard copy of articles with me if I find a few extra minutes in my day to read—when I'm waiting in line or for a meeting to start, for example. Lastly, because I'm a visual and kinesthetic learner, I benefit greatly from actively flipping pages and writing in the margins. If you learn similarly, you might find that hard copies (however bad for the planet) help you focus better, read faster, and retain more. Just make sure you recycle!

Regardless of whether you're using digital or hard copies, do whatever you can to eliminate distractions while reading. This can include eliminating clutter on or around your desk or relocating entirely to a place where you can focus.

Tip 2: Create a Distraction-free Environment

Distraction is the archnemesis of focus. Unfortunately, however, sometimes gaining control of your environment can be challenging, even after you silence your devices. For example, you may be working from a coffee shop or other shared space and can't control the surrounding sounds. Or perhaps you're working from home and may not be able (let alone want) to ignore a nearby housemate or family member. So, when your environment seems far from control, here are some tips for squeezing in a little extra quiet time.

- **Wake up an hour earlier.** Sometimes the early morning hours, when the rest of the world (or household) is still asleep, is the best time to focus on your studies. This time is perfect for the "larks" among us. Early risers, you know who you are.

- **Utilize the late evening.** If you're a night owl, this one's for you. Rather than turning on the tube for late-night laughs, crack open that textbook and crank out some homework. By this time in the evening, the phone calls and emails will have subsided, and as a night owl, your brain will be primed for analytical work. Of course, those who aren't night owls may not excel at productive work in the hours before bed, but this is an owl's time to shine.

- **Find a midday haven.** For the "third birds" (those who bristle at a 5 a.m. wake-up call but also like to get to bed at a decent hour), the lunch hour is yours for the taking. Schedule a conference room at your place of work or hit the local coffee shop to squeeze a solid hour of study into the workday.

- **Consider other options.** If none of the above work for you, eke out an extra 45–60 minutes of study time before or after work or classes. If you can't find a quiet place in your home or office where you won't be disturbed, pop into a nearby cafe instead. The best part is that you'll probably miss rush-hour traffic!

Don't take these opportunities for an extra hour or two of study for granted. As my former boss, Mauricio Umansky (celebrity CEO and husband of *Real Housewives* star Kyle Richards), once told me, "There are 24 hours in a day: eight hours for sleep, eight hours for work, and eight hours for play." Even if you only have two hours left after all your work is done, that's *still* two available hours. So start making a habit of investing time you would typically fritter away.

Tip 3: Find Hidden Time

If you're still having trouble finding time in your schedule to study, try completing a time journal for a week or two. (See the example below or use the full-sized version provided at the end of this book.) Record everything you do each day in thirty-minute increments, then color code your activities as follows:

- **Green** for essential tasks: work, sleep, class time, etc.
- **Yellow** for non-essential but important tasks like exercising or cleaning.
- **Red** for non-essential tasks such as watching your favorite show or scrolling through social media.

I've done this exercise myself and was surprised by what it revealed. The wonderful thing about the time journal is it helps you visualize pockets of time you're not using fully. The red activities are obvious time-wasters, but the time log reveals that even the most prudent time managers have room to grow.

Consider the yellow category, for instance. Sure, it's important to wash dishes, but do you have to partake in this activity *every* night? A professor teaching an intensive writing course once posed the same question to the class after we completed the time log. He suggested switching to disposable plates and cutlery during a month-long writing sprint. At first, I thought he was crazy, but after testing his approach, I realized I saved at least 30 minutes a day that I could redirect toward my novel. For the sake of the environment, however, I wouldn't suggest paper plates as a long-term strategy. We all get stuck in a rut from time to time, thinking we can only do things in a certain way or at a specific time. The purpose of the time log is to open our eyes to how we spend our time and to help us make more intentional decisions on how to invest that time.

Now let's look at a few more time-saving alternatives to yellow activities. While not many enjoy doing housework, it still needs to be done. But can you pay someone to clean your house during the busiest times of the semester? Or, if you're a parent, can you divide the housework among your children as part of their weekly chores? What about exercise? Can you work out at home using one of the many home workout apps or online memberships and save time driving to the gym each day? Can you bike to work and thereby multitask during your commute?

I'd also like you to reevaluate green activities and ask yourself if they are all truly essential and if they are tasks only you can do. For instance, getting your kids to school every day is necessary, but do *you* have to drive them *every* day? Or could you organize a carpool with your neighbors or ask a friend or family member to help out instead?

These ideas are just some alternatives to consider. And I encourage you to study your time log and think creatively about turning the red, yellow, and maybe even green time blocks in your week into additional hours of focused study. If you take the time to analyze your schedule, I'm confident

NOTES

you'll find opportunities to better steward the greatest gift of all: time.

Time Management Sheet

Time	Monday	Tuesday	Wednesday	Thursday	Friday	Saturday	Sunday
5:00							
5:30							
6:00							
6:30							
7:00							
7:30							
8:00							
8:30							
9:00							
9:30							
10:00							
10:30							
11:00							
11:30							
12:00							
12:30							
1:00							
1:30							
2:00							
2:30							
3:00							
3:30							
4:00							
4:30							
5:00							
5:30							
6:00							
6:30							
7:00							
7:30							
8:00							
8:30							
9:00							
9:30							
10:00							
10:30							
11:00							
11:30							

Tip 4: Plan Your Time

You've probably heard the saying, "Measure twice. Cut once." The same principle of thoughtful planning applies to your time, especially when you only have a few minutes. Adequate planning not only saves you time in the long run;

it also makes the time you spend more meaningful. Think back to the "highest-value" concept we discussed earlier. The purpose of your time-planning process should be to prioritize the critical tasks and assignments you identified in Chapter 2.

During this planning process, you should not only determine what work to complete, but also when you'll take breaks. Finding the optimal mix of focused concentration and rest periods for your body and brain is essential to maximizing your study time. There are a couple different models you can use to plan your time.

The first is the Pomodoro method, attributed to Francesco Cirillo,[11] in which you focus on a task for 25 minutes, then take a 5-minute break. In my opinion, this technique is suitable for "sprinting" or accomplishing many smaller tasks that don't require maximum concentration. For example, I might use this method to complete academic planning activities. For instance, I could devote 25 minutes to calendaring all upcoming deadlines for my current courses, 25 minutes to reviewing my homework assignments for the week, and another 25 minutes to preliminary research for a forthcoming paper—all with 5-minute breaks in between. This technique will keep me from spending too much time on any one activity, and the shorter "sprints" help me stay focused on a single task without getting overwhelmed or distracted by work that doesn't need to be accomplished today.

> *In fact, some data show that the optimal work-to-rest ratio for productivity is 52 minutes of work with a 17-minute break.*

However, my preferred method for getting into flow is to block off much longer intervals for focused work, with short breaks in between. In fact, some data show that the optimal work-to-rest ratio for productivity is 52 minutes of work with a 17-minute break[12]. While I usually prefer two hours of focused work before a break, building up your brain's stamina takes practice. Therefore, I suggest starting with smaller intervals (30 minutes to an hour) and building up to roughly 90 minutes of focused effort. And don't forget to take breaks between work sessions. Even "microbreaks" to stand, stretch, or shift your gaze from your screen to an object at a distance can benefit your mind and body.

Microbreak Activity:
Look up the "20-20-20 rule." Now try it.

Great. Now that you've had a brief break, you're in peak condition to test what you've learned so far.

POP QUIZ

You have 75 minutes before class starts, and the following assignment is due. You haven't started any of your homework yet. What do you do? Write your answer in the space below. Remember, the clock is ticking, so you only have 30 seconds to complete your response. Go!

Assignment:

Read Chapters 4–5 in the text. Be prepared for the in-class discussion questions (located in the syllabus). Homework Assignment #2, a one-page response paper, is due before class.

_____
_____
_____
_____
_____
_____

We'll return to the pop quiz later, but right now, I want to share my final recommendation for getting the most out of your time in school: embrace professionalism.

Always Be Professional

Treating your schoolwork as a job will help infuse the necessary discipline into your studies *and* pay dividends when things don't go according to plan. Here are some ways to demonstrate academic poise.

- ✓ **Get dressed for class,** even if it's online.
- ✓ **Arrive a few minutes early.** Don't be late!
- ✓ **Check your posture** during lectures—no slouching.
- ✓ **Demonstrate engagement** through active listening and positive participation.
- ✓ **Focus fully.** Put your phone away, and don't surf the web. Online shopping can wait.
- ✓ **Follow your professor's guidelines.** Submit assignments on time. Don't ask for extensions or exceptions to the rules. Adhere to submission guidelines, such as style, font, margins, assignment length, citations, etc.
- ✓ **Act with Integrity.** Don't cheat or plagiarize. Do your own work.
- ✓ **Own your mistakes and learn from them.** If you miss an assignment or perform poorly on an exam, don't make excuses for yourself, or argue about your grade. Instead, ask what you can do better!

If you're a working professional with a family, the likelihood of one of your other priorities taking precedence during the semester is high. For example, you may have to travel for a work-related trip or care for an ill child. Rest assured, if you've set a precedent of professional behavior and demonstrated that you value your studies, you'll be better able to navigate these types of setbacks. Let me give you a few examples.

What to Do When You Miss Class

Let's say you can't make class because you're out of town on a business trip. If it's a small class section, and you can't make one session, send a brief note to your professor as you would to your manager if you couldn't make an important meeting. Below is a sample email I might send to my professor to inform him of my absence in advance.

Dear Professor Baker,
I won't be able to make it to class this Thursday because I'm out of town for work, but I'll be sure to get the session notes from a classmate. I've attached the assignment that's due to this email. If I need to do anything else to catch up, please let me know.

Thank you and see you next week!
C

To be clear, you don't have to do this. But my guess is if you do, you'll probably hear back from your professor (especially if it's a small class), not only wishing you safe travels, but sharing any special discussion topics for the week or additional information you need to know. Once as an MBA student, when I extended this courtesy, a professor even offered me an alternative assignment to complete so I could still receive participation points for that week.

Before becoming a consultant, I worked as an academic administrator for a top-tier graduate school, and I can't tell you how many emails I received from professors asking about students who had missed classes. I know this may come as a shock, but most teachers do care about their students. They not only worry about your personal wellbeing when you're absent; they also worry about your ability to catch up with your studies when you return.

As a professor, I hated doling out bad grades, and as an academic administrator, I saw that the faculty I worked with felt the same way. Educators want students to perform well. Your success is their success. They want to know that you're learning and engaged. And if you demonstrate that you care too, you might just get that extra little bit of grace you need in a pinch. Now, let's take a look at another example.

What to Do if You Miss an Assignment

If you've followed the advice in this book, then you've planned ahead for all major assignments, but let's say an emergency arises. Work is exceptionally hectic, you've been putting in overtime all week, and you simply can't finish your homework on time. What should you do? Well, if I were you, I would still complete the assignment, even if I had to turn it in late—and even if I wouldn't receive any academic credit whatsoever. Why? Because my goal is to learn, and that assignment will probably help me with projects or exams in the future. Below is a sample email demonstrating how I would handle the situation.

Dear Professor Baker,
Unfortunately, I missed the deadline for last week's assignment, but I completed it anyway, just for practice. I know it's late, and I won't receive any points, but would you mind taking a

NOTES

look at the attached assignment anyway? I would appreciate any feedback you can offer. Thank you so much.

See you in class!
C

I admit that even as a prudent planner, I had to send an email like this as a fully-employed MBA student. Unfortunately, despite our earnest preparation, unavoidable circumstances sometimes arise. Still, if you've shown yourself to be someone who consistently takes your education seriously, most professors will meet you halfway. I've said this before, but it bears repeating. Your instructors want to see you succeed. They want you to understand the material, and they want to guide you through the learning process—that's why they became educators in the first place.

Now back to the email. Did you notice how I didn't ask for an exception to the rules? I also didn't make any excuses or offer a long-winded story. Instead, I stated the facts and asked nicely for feedback that would help me improve. If you follow this approach too, the outcome might surprise you. Maybe you'll receive partial credit for the assignment, or perhaps even full credit (as I did)—provided you keep that information to yourself!

What to Do When You're Late for Class

First, don't be late!

Second, if an unavoidable emergency occurs (let's say the freeway gets shut down, which happened to me once) keep your wits about you. Drive safely and slip into class quietly. If you consistently show up early and you're late to class once, your professor will probably give you the benefit of the doubt.

So, what happened when I was an hour-and-a-half late to a three-hour class because the freeway shut down? Well, first, I debated whether to go at all, mainly because my professor was a surly woman who swore she locked the door after the first five minutes of class so latecomers wouldn't interrupt her brilliant lectures. But here's the thing: her lessons *were* brilliant! In fact, they were so good I didn't want to miss the rest of class that day, so I swallowed my pride and, risking humiliation, attempted to slip into class during the break. I took a seat in the back row and prepared to take notes.

I thought I had successfully flown under the radar until my professor pulled me aside after class. I was sure I had a stern chiding in store, but do you know what Professor McGruff said? Before I could open my mouth to explain the mess on the freeway, she thanked me for my professionalism and for "not making a big fuss" when I walked in the door. She already knew about the freeway fiasco, but I apologized anyway. I also told Ms. McGruff the truth—that I didn't want to miss her lecture because I was learning so much in her class. Do you know what she did next? The toughest, gruffest professor in my program opened her notebook and let me copy her outline from the first half of class, word-for-word.

I was floored. However, when I later became an adjunct professor at the same college, I understood her reaction because I rooted for every student in my class too. I wanted them to do well, learn, and achieve mastery. It pained me to give any grade lower than a *C*, and I would have gladly offered extra office hours to help any of my students. The problem is, though, as students, we're often afraid to ask for help when we need it.

Every academic institution is different, but they all have some level of student support, as well as accommodations for students with learning disabilities. If you're struggling in any way, personally or academically, don't be afraid to reach out to an administrator or instructor and ask for help. Please know they are on your side and want you to succeed.

What to Do When You're Stumped

It's your instructor's job to teach and your job to learn—and that means taking an active role in the learning process. So, if you don't understand something, the onus is on *you* to figure it out. Use your resources (textbooks, readings, your library's database), ask your peers, and scour the internet until you find an answer. If you've done your homework (literally and figuratively) and still have questions, then it's perfectly fine to reach out to your professor or teacher's assistant. I've had to do this a few times and, almost without exception, the response I received was, "That's a great question, and I'll answer it in the next class session because other students are probably struggling with that too."

I include the above scenarios as examples of "professionalism" because I want you to get into the habit of managing your education the same way you should manage your career. Learning is an active process, and it's up to you to make the most of your education.

Pop Quiz Answer

Now, let's get back to that pop quiz question. Below is how I would answer. You may have responded differently, and that's okay, provided you're using the techniques we discussed to maximize your output and optimize your effort.

First, I would read the homework assignment and the in-class discussion questions. Because the homework assignment is worth more than the discussion, I'd focus on that first. I'd give myself 15–20 minutes of focused reading on the assignment topic before tackling it. Because I already know the discussion questions, if I came across anything that relates to them in my reading, I'd highlight it for later. Then I'd give myself 30–40 minutes to prepare my written assignment. Thankfully, it's only one page, so I'd take a couple of seconds to jot down a simple outline following the five-paragraph essay model. Once written, I'd check for spelling and re-read for accuracy before submitting.

With the 20–30 minutes I have remaining, I'd skim the two chapters for the discussion topics (highlighting related material). Then I would work through the "rock star reading" steps to at least review the introduction, conclusion, bold words, and graphics for both chapters while keeping an eye out for any of the topics from the class discussion questions.

Here's the most important part: Whatever homework I didn't finish before class, I'd complete as soon as possible afterward. The trick to staying on top of things is never to get too far behind to begin with because a critical part of the learning process is the ability to build new ideas on top of existing ones. You'll find that as the semester progresses, your understanding grows and deepens in complexity. As a student, skipping too many readings, assignments, or class sessions creates significant gaps in your learning structure. Think of your learning as a Jenga block tower—the more you progress in the course and attempt to build on a porous foundation, the more likely your understanding will crumble. So don't get discouraged if you miss something (a class, an assignment, a quiz, etc.). Just shake it off and get right back in the game. The fewer missing pieces in your Jenga learning tower, the better it will hold up under pressure!

Part II

The Busy Student's Guide
to
Academic Writing

CHAPTER 7

Before You Begin

"I write to discover what I know."
~ FLANNERY O'CONNOR

Whether you're an undergrad, graduate, or even an art student, chances are you'll be asked to practice your writing skills by structuring and composing academic papers. While some universities currently allow students to use generative artificial intelligence (AI) to draft essays, the process of writing teaches students how to think critically, organize their thoughts, take a position, and defend it logically. These skills are timeless, and for that reason, I've included this section on scholarly writing in this book. Academic writing can take many forms, including descriptive, analytical, persuasive, and critical. Let's start by taking a brief look at the different types of academic writing. Then, we'll review various reference sources for your paper. After we've covered these foundational elements, you'll be ready to begin the research and writing process.

Types of Academic Writing

Below are the most common forms of academic writing. Bear in mind, however, some assignments may require a combination of the following types.

Descriptive

Descriptive writing is the simplest, most foundational form of writing and is used to summarize information or report facts. For example, if your professor asks you to summarize an article or describe the outcome of an experiment, you would use descriptive writing.

I also include reflective essays in this category because they require you to *describe* your response to an experience (field trip, site visit, panel discussion, play, poem, painting, musical composition, or another creative or artistic expression).

> You'll know your instructor is looking for descriptive writing if the assignment instructions ask you to **define, identify, report,** or **summarize** information.

Analysis

Analytical writing builds on descriptive writing but takes it a step further by requiring you to organize information into groups or categories. When I think of analysis, I imagine breaking a big idea down into smaller components or parts. "Compare and contrast" papers fit into this category because they usually involve comparing one concept or theory to another, topic by topic.

If your assignment asks you to **analyze, compare, contrast, relate,** or **examine** information, you will likely need to engage your analytical writing skills.

Persuasive

Persuasive writing includes both description and analysis, but it also requires you to express a point of view based on your factual analysis. Your perspective can take the form of an argument, evaluation, interpretation, or recommendation, but the evidence presented in the paper must always support it.

When you see the words "**evaluate**," "**defend**," "**recommend**," or "**take a position**," you'll know you need to flex your persuasive writing powers.

Critical

Critical (or research) writing assignments combine all of the above writing types but go even further by asking you to consider at least two points of view (one of which can be your own). For example, a critical writing assignment may ask you to critique a journal article, evaluate an argument or data interpretation, and perhaps even provide your own argument or interpretation.

If your professor asks you to **critique**, **debate**, or **evaluate** a work, your assignment likely requires critical writing.

Putting It Together

A simple way to organize your paper is to think of the hierarchy of writing types as an outline for your paper's sequence. Let's use critical writing as an example. Typically, you should start by *describing* the topic, situation, theory, or idea. Next, you'll want to dive further into the subject area by *analyzing* it—that is, breaking it into parts. If you're presenting more than one point of view, you'll want to examine both sides of the argument. Then, based on that analysis, you'll draw a conclusion and attempt to *persuade* your audience to agree with your point of view.

> This process supports the following writing structure, which we'll explore in the next chapter: Introduction → Background → Analysis → Conclusion/ Recommendation.

Now, let's go back to Bloom's Taxonomy in Appendix B. Notice how each level of writing represents upward movement on the pyramid, from "recall" (or description) through analysis and evaluation until you reach the point where you develop your own arguments ("creation"). The pyramid's highest levels are supported by a foundation of facts and evidence you've summarized, synthesized, organized, and reorganized to create something new. That's why the writing process is so important and often challenging. Effective composition demonstrates the evolution of your understanding and is evidence of your mastery of the subject at hand.

Understanding Source Material

The research process can often seem overwhelming, especially given the amount of information available on most topics. The following tips will help you understand the types of sources available, when to use them, and how to curate the highest quality references for your paper.

Peer-Reviewed Research

While it's perfectly fine to google topics during the brainstorming process and read internet articles and blog posts to get a quick overview of a potential area of interest, I would avoid citing these in your research paper. Superficial internet research is acceptable when you want to get background information or a quick understanding of different subject areas, but once you define your topic, you should only cite peer-reviewed articles, primary-source information, and other reputable sources in your paper to support your thesis.

So what is peer-reviewed research? A peer-reviewed article is written by an expert or team of experts (professors, scientists, physicians, and other researchers), reviewed by fellow experts, and selected for publication in a scholarly trade journal. Because such articles are written and reviewed by subject-matter experts, they hold the highest merit within the hierarchy of published works.

The best place to find scholarly research is typically in your college or university library database. (Google Scholar isn't bad either.) Educational institutions pay for access to many types of reference resources and materials, so be sure to take full advantage of the information available to you through your institution.

Pro Tip: Librarians are one of the most underutilized assets in colleges and universities. They typically have a wealth of knowledge about available materials and databases and are more than happy to point you in the right direction. (Some are so enthusiastic they even do the research for you—but don't tell them I said that!) For this reason, I highly recommend you make friends with your school's library staff. Show respect for their policies and gratitude for their assistance, and you'll discover what an asset your local librarian can be.

Now that you know what type of reference material to focus on (i.e., peer-reviewed research), let's do a quick overview of the hierarchy of information and when to use each type of resource.

The Information Hierarchy

Academic articles, books, and industry white papers. The best research sources are articles from peer-reviewed academic journals, traditionally published books, and well-researched whitepapers. Support for your thesis should come primarily from these materials, and you'll typically find them in your library's databases. The section above explains why these are the best sources of scholastic research. Now let's look at other types of source material.

News articles. If your paper is about a historical or current event, then citing news publications is appropriate. Just be sure the article is from a legitimate news source (a reputable international, national, or regional newspaper). Journalistic sources may also be used for your paper's "background" section. However, be cautious of lesser-known news publications and websites. The best news sources have longevity and a history of adhering to ethical journalistic practices. In my opinion, the best way to search news articles is through your university's library database because you can easily identify and sort articles from the world's top news agencies there.

Internet resources (Wikipedia, blog posts, various news articles). These sources can be helpful for an overview of a topic or background information. You can use them when researching potential paper topic ideas. However, I don't recommend citing blog posts unless they are published by well-known, reputable organizations (often nonprofit third parties) considered industry leaders. Be wary of blog posts that use information to sell or promote a product or service. Though many internet blogs appear to be sources of unbiased information, most actually exist as "advertorials" to generate views and ad revenue, receiving commissions on the products and services they promote. While no information is ever completely unbiased, you should seek third-party sources that have a reputation for being fair, balanced, and knowledgeable.

As you evaluate research material, remember that we live in a world where anyone can write and publish just about anything online in a matter of seconds. Therefore, understanding the hierarchy of information, the difference between primary and secondary sources, and journalistic standards will help you become a more thoughtful information consumer.

Primary versus Secondary Sources

Primary sources. These are original creations (documents, images, maps, artifacts, artwork, etc.) or contemporaneous, first-hand accounts of historical events. Examples include a newspaper report by someone who witnessed an event or interviewed people who did, as well as contemporaneous narratives documented in diaries, letters, interviews, and speeches. Primary sources can also include text from laws and other government documents, emails, and original research. Datasets, survey data (such as census information), and other economic statistics are also considered primary resources.

Secondary sources. Secondary sources are one step removed from primary sources and typically quote or reference them. Secondary sources usually interpret or analyze a historical event, period, or creative work. Examples include most books, research data analysis or interpretation, and articles about a subject by authors not directly involved with the original topic, work, or research.

NOTES

Please note this discussion has more nuances than we can explore in this book. For example, the same resource may be considered a primary source in one instance and a secondary source in another. Nevertheless, the purpose of this discussion is to encourage you to use as much primary source information as possible and to consider how far removed your supporting material is from the original research, data, or event.

While reading expert analysis is important, don't let endless internet musings on William Blake or Ludwig van Beethoven substitute for a thorough submersion into Blake's poetry or Beethoven's concertos. Even though writing a paper on poetry you haven't read sounds silly, if you're not careful in your research and mindful of your sources, an articulate analysis can devolve into an inaccurate game of "telephone." Review the original source, research, or dataset whenever you can, and then use secondary sources to supplement and support your own thorough analysis. I've found on a number of occasions that my interpretation of an original work or dataset differs greatly from that of the author I've reviewed in a secondary source. As a critical thinker and writer, you are an investigator. Not only are you collecting others' interpretations, but you're also seeking to determine the facts that will enable you to craft your own narrative, one supported by the strongest evidence available.

Publication Standards and Ethics

You may wonder why I've spent so much time describing the various types of media, and it's because different standards of accountability apply to each. Let's take a moment to consider traditional journalism. When I was a communications student in college, I studied journalistic standards and ethics. These principles were later reinforced when I worked for the local newspaper. For example, for every story I wrote, I was required to gather primary source information, which included interviewing experts, attending and reporting on town hall meetings, and sourcing quotes from eyewitnesses of local news events. Later, when I wrote for online news publications, including *The Huffington Post*, even though the medium was digital rather than print, I was still required to conduct primary-source interviews, and my stories (even those written on the *HuffPost* blog) were fact-checked prior to publication. In addition, I was also required to submit citations and references.

Below are seven standards typical of high-quality journalism.[13]

- **Multiple Credible Sources**: These may include eyewitnesses, officials, and experts.
- **Avoidance of Bias**: Present facts and necessary context in a fair, balanced, and dispassionate manner.
- **Documentation**: This can include reports, studies, data, videos, photos, and audio recordings.
- **Fairness**: Treat sources with appropriate respect, giving subjects a chance to share their points of view or respond to any assertions or allegations.
- **Verification**: Check and confirm all reported facts and details.
- **Balance**: Represent multiple sides of an issue, event, or controversy without giving undue weight or legitimacy to one side or point of view.
- **Context**: Present the facts in a way that is honest, fair, and accurate.

In addition to these standards of quality, the journalism industry also traditionally upholds certain ethical standards. Below is a summary of the Society of Professional Journalists' Code of Ethics.[14]

NOTES

- Seek truth and report it.
- Minimize harm.
- Act independently.
- Be accountable and transparent.

While journalists are people just like us, with their own opinions and biases, it's important to understand the standards the profession at large seeks to uphold. Additionally, traditional book publishers also uphold stringent standards for non-fiction works and require rigorous fact-checking prior to publication. Now, compare the above rigor and standards to the average, unsubstantiated content that frequently appears on the internet. When you know the ideal standards for published content, you'll be better able to discern the information that doesn't measure up.

I share this information so you can better understand the many source materials available to you. While I believe most types of content have a time and place, when writing an academic research paper, you need to be sure you use only the highest-quality, most relevant resources available.

CHAPTER 8

Prewriting

"You can make anything by writing."

~ C. S. LEWIS

The Academic Writing Process

Following is a guide for writing academic papers. You may notice some study skills concepts are repeated, and that's because the principles of planning, preparation, and execution apply across disciplines. Below, I've summarized the primary steps in the writing process. In the next pages, we'll look at each step in greater detail, so grab a pen, pencil, or highlighter, and get ready to do some active reading.

Writing Process Overview

——————————Prewriting——————————

Step 1	Step 2	Step 3	Step 4	Step 5
Planning	Research & Notetaking	Outlining	Writing & Revising	Reviewing & Proofing

——————Writing & Editing——————

The Prewriting Process

The prewriting process is composed of planning, researching, and outlining. Let's begin with the planning phase.

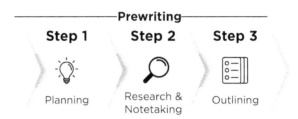

Step 1: Planning

Start by reading the instructions. Determine the assignment's length and type (reflection, research, analysis, etc.). You'll need to take these requirements into account when selecting your topic. Also, review the citation style and grading criteria or rubric, and make notes about any specific requirements for the paper's content.

Next, calendar key dates. Has the instructor indicated a deadline for topic selection, initial research, an outline, or a rough draft? If so, add those dates to your calendar now, along with one or two reminders (as discussed in Chapter 2).

If only the final paper has a due date, with no other checkpoints, then you'll need to create your own accountability. First, calendar the final deadline, then block off several full days to devote to the paper. (If you're a working student, you'll probably want to select specific weekends.) Decide what you want to accomplish in each of these "binge-working" sessions.

Now, create your own internal deadlines. For example, select target dates to complete your research, an outline, and a first draft. Then, calendar those dates, adding reminders a few days prior to each deadline. Lastly, schedule "final deadline" reminders on your calendar several weeks and days before the paper is due to ensure you're not caught off guard at the last minute. Multiple reminders may seem like overkill, but if you're a busy student with a lot going on, it's just as easy to miss a reminder as it is to sleep through an alarm when you're exhausted. Effective planning strategies create space for the unexpected, so you don't always feel like you're hanging on by a thread.

Now let's review those key dates again, and this time, I'll show you how to create your own project timeline. Personally, I like to start with the final deadline and work my way back from there. I use this "reverse timeline" approach for all major projects, including my writing projects.

Therefore, a sample timeline for a research paper might look like this:

Research Paper Sample Timeline

September 15 - 30	*Research Paper Topics*
October 1	*Determine Topic*
October 1 - 31	*Research & Take Notes*
October 21	*Complete Outline*
November 1	*Complete Rough Draft*
December 1	*Complete Second Draft*
December 10	*Research Paper Due*

NOTES

Note that the bolded line items are deadlines I would enter into my calendar (with a reminder) to ensure they're not missed. Once you have your key deadlines, you can also calendar specific blocks of time to work on each task within the larger project. For example, if I were writing a research paper due at the end of the term, I'd want to spend a couple of weekends at the library (in person or virtually) to conduct research. I'll also want a couple of days of uninterrupted writing to complete my drafts. Here's what that schedule might look like. Note that by blocking off these sessions in my calendar, I ensure I have ample time to complete the project, and I'm not scrambling at the last minute to find time to work on my paper.

Research Paper Timeline

	Sunday	Monday	Tuesday	Wednesday	Thursday	Friday	Saturday
OCTOBER							*research* *10 a.m. — 2 p.m.*
	1	**2**	**3**	**4**	**5**	**6**	7 *research* *10 a.m. — 2 p.m.*
	8 *research* *10 a.m. — 2 p.m.*	**9**	**10**	**11**	**12**	**13**	14 *research, draft outline* *10 a.m. — 3 p.m.*
	15	**16**	**17**	**18**	**19**	**20**	21
	22	**23** *work on rough draft* *10 a.m. — 4 p.m.*	**24**	**25**	**26**	**27**	28
	29	**30**	**31**				
NOVEMBER				*complete rough draft* *10 a.m. — 4 p.m.* **1**	**2**	**3**	4
	5	**6**	**7**	**8** *revise 1st half* *10 a.m. — 2 p.m.*	**9**	**10**	11
	12	**13**	**14** *revise 2nd half* *10 a.m. — 2 p.m.*	**15**	**16**	**17**	18
	19	**20**	**21**	**22**	**23** *complete 2nd draft* *10 a.m. — 2 p.m.*	**24**	25
	26	**27**	**28**	**29**	**30**		
DECEMBER						**1**	2
	final touches *10 a.m. — 2 p.m.* 3 *research paper due*	**4**	**5**	**6**	*proofread* *10 a.m. — 1 p.m.* **7**	**8**	9
	10	**11**	**12**	**13**	**14**	**15**	16

Begin brainstorming topics. As you consider a subject's scope, you'll want to take the required length and paper type into account to ensure that your topic is sufficiently broad (and appropriately narrow) to meet the paper's requirements.

Some helpful factors in determining the topic's scope include 1) the assignment's page count, 2) use of specific analytical tools or frameworks, 3) any compare/contrast requirements, and 4) policy recommendations, opinions, next steps, or other final conclusions required.

Perhaps the biggest challenge, however, is selecting a topic that is appropriately narrow. If you choose a subject that is too broad, not only will the available research overwhelm you, but you'll also risk writing a paper that lacks the appropriate depth of analysis.

If you're struggling to come up with a topic, I suggest flipping through your textbook or other reading materials for topics of interest. Sidebars and case studies can be a good starting point. Current events, news articles, and industry publications are also excellent sources of inspiration. Additionally, if you've taken my previous advice and subscribed to newsletters or podcasts related to your studies, you'll find a continuous stream of ideas for further exploration in your daily feed and inbox.

Because term papers require a lot of time and effort, finding a topic that truly interests you is worthwhile. If you're a working student, think about a topic you could turn into a report for your manager that might benefit the organization or that you could showcase in a job interview. (Hey, if you can get an *A* on your paper *and* a promotion, why not go the extra mile?) The more interested in the topic you are, the harder you'll work, and sometimes that extra bit of intrinsic motivation is exactly what you need to take your paper to the next level.

Now select a topic. When selecting a topic, work from big to small. Start with a big idea and then narrow it down according to the assignment guidelines. At this stage, your initial cursory research will confirm two things: 1) that the topic is broad enough to meet the paper's requirements and 2) that the topic has sufficient peer-reviewed research to support your thesis.

Once you've selected a topic or two of interest, do a quick search for academic articles to see what's already been written. Since you'll only want to include peer-reviewed journals and reputable periodicals in your research, you need to be sure that enough of those sources exist on your topic. As you scroll through your library's database, you'll also get a greater sense of the subcategories within your selected subject area. These subcategories will likely help you hone in even more on your potential thesis.

What you don't want to do at this stage is fall in love with a topic idea only to find there isn't enough research available for you to craft a compelling report or strongly supported thesis, so this "pre-research" step is essential. If you find any particularly noteworthy articles during this preliminary search, be sure to download and save them immediately. Nothing is worse than going down the search engine rabbit hole and then being unable to find that "perfect" article when you need it later on. It only takes a few minutes to bookmark a handful of articles, and this step will save you a lot of time and frustration in the long run.

After conducting your preliminary research, you'll probably have a working thesis in mind. This governing thought will likely transform and become even more refined as you continue to research and eventually become an expert on your topic. Now let's do a quick review of what we just learned about the academic writing planning process.

NOTES

THE PLANNING PROCESS
1. **Read the instructions.** Determine the paper's length and type.
2. **Calendar key dates.** Include one or two reminders prior to each critical deadline.
3. **Brainstorm and select a topic.** Use the assignment guidelines to determine the appropriate topic and scope. Write about topics that interest you.

Step 2: Research and Notetaking

Though you should be researching and taking notes simultaneously, I've separated these sections to provide greater clarity on each. We've already discussed high-quality sources for your paper, so now, let's look at methods for notetaking when reviewing your peer-reviewed research studies and academic articles.

There's more than one way to take notes. Below, I've included some of my favorites. The most important thing to remember, however, is to always connect your notes to their source; otherwise, you'll find yourself in a jam when trying to cite your work.

Notecards

Some experts suggest writing individual facts or quotes on separate notecards. The benefit of this approach is that it's easy to organize and reorganize information until it flows. The downside is that you may end up with a mountain of notecards and spend a lot of unnecessary time transferring information from one place to another.

To see the effective use of the notecard methodology in action, check out the video on Ryan Holiday's notetaking system[15] linked on the Online Resources page of my website: https://www.get-the-degree.com/blog/get-the-degree-online-resources. His method involves the following steps:

1. Read and highlight information in the text
2. Review that information and select key ideas, stories, or quotes worth remembering
3. Write those ideas on individual notecards
4. Categorize each card and file it alphabetically by topic

This method is great if you want to amass an archive of data to reference throughout the years and across bodies of work.

The Cornell Method

The Cornell notetaking system is a way of taking, organizing, and reviewing notes. This system works well for handwritten notes, and any sheet of paper can be adapted for the Cornell method. You start by dividing your notetaking sheet into three sections: a 2.5-inch column on the far left, a 6-inch column on the right, and a 2 x 8.5-inch row at the bottom of the page. (Picture an upside-down "T" on the page.)

The widest column is where you jot down your notes as you read or listen to a lecture. In the more slender left-hand column, you organize your notes by listing main ideas, questions, keywords, or other study prompts. Finally, the bottom section is completed after the reading or lecture; this space provides an opportunity to reflect on what you learned by writing a summary.

Pro Tip: To help you put this method into practice, I've included a few Cornell-style note pages at the back of this book. You can even use these note pages as a study aid by folding the right side of the page over to cover the detailed notes, while leaving the subject or key term visible on the left. Pretty genius, right?

NOTES

Your Own Words

This third approach is my favorite. Typically, I start by reading and highlighting a text. Then, when I'm done reading, I review my notes and summarize the article in my own words, focusing on the areas that specifically pertain to my thesis. The reason I like this approach so much is twofold.

First, it's almost impossible to plagiarize when you restate ideas in your own words. Furthermore, as we've discussed, doing so ensures you understand the material and aren't just repeating it verbatim. Some interesting research by Daniel Oppenheimer of Princeton University shows that when students use complex language unnecessarily in college essays, it undermines their credibility and intelligence. In his article, Oppenheimer reveals that simple texts were given higher marks than both moderately and highly complex texts—regardless of the quality of the essay.[16] The bottom line is that simple passages are easier to read, even for your professors, so think about that the next time you're tempted to pepper your paper with erudite vernacular. (Get my point?) But what if I come across a particularly compelling quote that I might want to use in my paper? In that case, I'm sure to put it in quotations and include a page number in my notes, so I'll have everything I need to properly cite it later.

Second, summarizing an article after I read it means it's still fresh in my mind, and therefore it's easier to remember the key points. If I skip this step after my research session, I find myself rereading articles because I've forgotten their contents. Immediately jotting down important points saves time and boosts comprehension.

If I follow this approach for every piece of research, my digital notes document hosts a list of every article I've read, followed by a summary or bullets with key points from the reading. By organizing my notes this way, I never have to wonder where I read a particular theory or quote because every bullet point is arranged by article. If I need to separate my notes by topic, I'll typically highlight topic areas in a specific color and then group them together when I start drafting my paper.

Color Coding

Another great idea is to code notes from each source with different font colors. This way, when you cut and paste your notes into your rough draft, you always know exactly where each idea originated. Now that's a colorful idea!

Below are a few key themes across the different styles of notetaking.

NOTETAKING TAKE-AWAYS

- Highlight and record key ideas, statistics, and quotes.
- Always connect those ideas to their source (bonus points for recording page numbers).
- Summarize each important article in your own words. I sometimes scrawl key themes in large letters across the top of printed articles or in the margins for easy reference later.
- It doesn't matter which system you use as long as you are consistent. This will result in a smoother writing process.

Step 3: Outlining

Remember what you learned in Chapter 6: "Measure twice, cut once"? Well, that principle couldn't be more apt than when outlining your paper. Outlining is a way to plan and organize your work that saves time and brings greater clarity to your writing. In addition, an outline serves as the foundation for your paper's organizational structure. A well-organized treatise is far easier to read and understand than a disorganized stream of thoughts.

Pro Tip: If your professors can read your papers easily, they're more likely to give you a good grade.

Systems of Order

Two primary systems of order exist in writing: hierarchical and sequential. Outlining speaks primarily to the hierarchy of information—how groups (or categories) of information relate to one another within a greater system. An excellent example of hierarchical order is Kingdom Animalia, the system used to classify living things into distinct categories. Secondarily, outlines also address sequential order, typically relating to the sequence, or chronological order, of items, operations, or processes. You will consider the sequence of information presented in both your outline and drafted paper as you review and revise your work.

Now, let me offer an even easier way to think about an outline: a grocery list. Let's pretend you're going to the grocery store and don't have a lot of time, so you decide to organize your list based on specific grocery store zones. Since similar items are typically grouped together, you'll prepare your list based on food type or category—for instance: dairy, meat, grains, vegetables, and fruit. Now, let's say you want to take your groupings a step further and make your categories more granular by creating subcategories. Below is an example of what that might look like.

Grocery List "Outline"

I. Dairy
   A. Milk
      1. Nonfat milk
      2. 1% milk
   B. Cheese
      1. Cheddar
      2. Provolone
      3. Swiss

II. Meat
   A. Chicken
      1. Boneless, Skinless Breasts
      2. Bone-in Thighs
   B. Beef
      1. Tri Tip
      2. Ground

III. Grains
   A. Dried Grains
      1. Rice
         a. Jasmine
         b. Brown
      2. Quinoa
      3. Steel-cut Oats
   B. Loaf Bread
      1. Whole Wheat
      2. Sourdough
      3. Ciabatta
   C. Other Breads
      1. Bagels
      2. Muffins
   D. Pastries
      1. Croissants
      2. Donuts

NOTES

IV. Vegetables
- A. Asparagus
- B. Cucumber
- C. Zucchini
- D. Spinach

V. Fruit
- A. Fresh
  1. Stone Fruits
     a. Cherries
     b. Peaches
     c. Apricots
  2. Melons
     a. Watermelon
     b. Cantaloupe
     c. Honeydew
  3. Berries
     a. Blueberries
     b. Strawberries
     c. Raspberries
  4. Other
     a. Apples
     b. Oranges
     c. Bananas
- B. Dried
  1. Cranberries
  2. Raisins
  3. Apricots
  4. Apples
- C. Frozen
  1. Mangos
  2. Cherries
  3. Strawberries
  4. Blueberries

POP QUIZ

Are you starting to get the hang of it? If so, I have a couple questions for you.

1. Where in this outline would you list nondairy milk, for example, almond or oat milk?
2. Let's say I have a sweet tooth, and I forgot to include cookies on my list. Where should they go?
3. Lastly, would you organize anything in the outline differently? (Hint: Your answers to the questions above might inform this answer.)

Take a moment to review the outline and then write your answers in the space below.

1.

2.

3.

The more you practice outlining, you'll discover that sometimes you need to make a judgment call. Now let's look at some possible answers to the questions above.

1. I can think of a couple of places nondairy milk might be listed.
   - You could create a subcategory under "Dairy" that reads "Nondairy Items" and possibly change the first Roman numeral heading to "Dairy/Nondairy." See below.
   I. Dairy/Nondairy
      A. Milk
         1. Nonfat milk

2. 1% milk

B. Cheese

   1. Cheddar

   2. Provolone

   3. Swiss

C. Nondairy Items

   1. Almond milk

   2. Coconut yogurt

- You could also create an entirely new category called "Nondairy Items" (perhaps as Roman numeral "II") and list nondairy milk, yogurt, and ice cream under this category as shown below.

   II.   Nondairy Items

      A. Almond milk

      B. Coconut yogurt

      C. Oat milk ice cream

- Can you think of any other ways to categorize almond, soy, coconut, or oat milk?

2. As for cookies, you could create an additional subheading under "Grains," or you could create an entirely new Roman numeral for "Sweets." Are there other ways you could classify cookies as well? I'm sure there are. Perhaps you'd create a new category for "Bakery Items"? Take a moment to draft your revised shopping list, including cookies in the notes section to the left.

3. In addition to the revisions suggested above, I might also consider the following revisions to the initial outline. For example:

- I might consider separating breads from other grain products by creating a Roman numeral for "Breads" and removing all bread products from the rest of the "Grains" group. Looking back at the grocery list outline, what issues arise when you separate the grain group? How do you determine if these concerns are relevant? (Write your answer below.)

- Or perhaps, I would create a separate category for "Sweets"? But if so, would you move all pastries under that heading, or would you move donuts to sweets and leave croissants under the "Other Bread" or "Pastry" items? Would your answer change if the croissants were chocolate instead of plain? Why or why not?

- What about items within each subcategory? Would you organize those? And if so, would you alphabetize them or list them in order of importance? Or do you think their order doesn't matter? Whatever your opinion, write it in the space below.

If your brain is starting to hurt (or your stomach is growling), you're not alone. You can structure information in different ways, but your goal is to be clear and consistent.

> *You can structure information in different ways,*
> *but your goal is to be clear and consistent.*

If you notice you're struggling with the classification process, ask yourself if that could be a result of gaps in your learning. You may need to increase your knowledge base to accurately categorize information and organize your outline. Full disclosure: I spent more time researching bread products and fruit types for this chapter than I'd like to admit.

If you're still unsure how to classify specific sections of your outline or paper, go back to your thesis and ask which structure best supports your governing thought. In the grocery list example, my goal is to organize my list in a way that makes shopping easier. Therefore, if I needed to make a judgment call, I'd ultimately group questionable items by physical location rather than their official food group. You'll need to make similar organizational judgment calls, and considering how ideas support your thesis and flow logically and sequentially will help you make those decisions.

If all that talk about food hasn't made you pause to get a snack, let's now look at some common structures for academic writing.

Basic Logical Structuring

Whether you're writing a paragraph or a Ph.D. dissertation, basic logical structuring applies. You should start with a governing thought, or thesis. And that overarching hypothesis should be supported by a few main ideas or key points. Those ideas, in turn, should be bolstered by facts and evidence in the form of quotes, statistics, examples, and the like. Below is a visual representation of this model.

Research Paper Structure

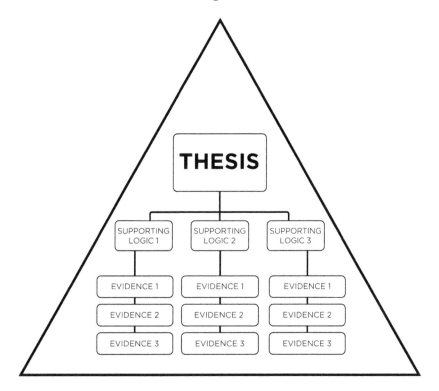

Standard Academic Paper Structures

Before you begin your outline, it's helpful to understand academic papers' general structures, so you can model yours accordingly. Below are two examples of standard research paper formats. However, please note that your instructor's specific requirements and formatting guidelines should trump everything else.

A standard research paper usually requires you to 1) introduce a topic or thesis, 2) discuss its background or historical context, 3) analyze relevant research, and 4) reach a final conclusion.

Standard Research Paper Format

I. Introduction
- Topic/Thesis
- Purpose and scope

II. Background
- Summarize topic background
- Provide historical context

III. Analysis
- Summarize relevant research/supporting facts
- Analyze research
- Make recommendations
- Explain potential future developments

IV. Conclusion
- Restate major findings
- Present final conclusions

Problem-Solution Papers

If you're asked to analyze a specific problem or issue, the format is a little different. It looks more like this.

1. **Introduction.** First, you'll articulate the problem and state your thesis. If the issue is particularly complex (climate change, for instance), you may want to communicate which aspects of the subject the paper will address and provide a "roadmap" for the report's upcoming sections.

2. **Background.** Next, you'll want to include any historical material that provides the necessary context for understanding the analysis. You may also want to offer a brief chronology of the issue, beginning with the problem's genesis and bringing the reader to the current, or status quo, approach.

3. **Analysis.** You will then analyze the nature of the problem, as well as future ramifications, and propose a potential solution or solutions. If offering more than one, you may then want to critique (or compare and contrast) these different approaches.

4. **Recommendation/Conclusion.** For this type of paper, your professor will likely ask you to take a position by recommending the best solution to the problem. Therefore, you will conclude with your recommendation based on the evidence and analysis you presented in your essay.

Below is an example of an outline for this type of paper.

Standard Format for Addressing Issue or Problem

I. Introduction
- Articulate topic, issue, or problem
- State thesis
- Present roadmap for following sections

II. Background
- Summarize relevant historical material
- Explain genesis of issue → developments → status quo

III. Analysis
- Describe nature of current problem/ramifications
- Propose and explain solution

IV. Conclusion
- Summarize problem, proposal, viability, and ramifications of solution
- Restate final conclusion/resolution

While the overall structure of a general research paper and an issue/problem paper are largely the same, the latter describes the nature or origin of the problem and then offers a critical look at potential solutions.

General Guidelines

Your paper's outline and structure should resemble the professor's guidelines as closely as possible. Therefore, I would start with the general structures presented above and then refine your headings and subheadings based on the specific paper parameters and grading criteria your professor provided.

Pro Tip: Your professors shouldn't have to search for the required information. In fact, they probably won't. If you know your instructor wants a detailed historical account of an issue and three potential solutions, make those content areas impossible to miss with headings such as "History of the Issue" and "Potential Solutions." Then, provide a numbered list with the three solutions you propose. Finally, scan your paper for all the assigned requirements. Can you easily locate those items based on your report's organizational structure, table of contents, and skillfully separated sections and subsections? If not, go back to your outline and reorganize until every section is clear and flows in a logical progression.

THE PURPOSE OF AN OUTLINE

1. Helps focus your research and writing
2. Creates an orderly, logical structure that facilitates the reader's understanding of the topic

---

Your outline is designed to be a guide for your research and writing. It helps you stay on track. As the body of your paper fleshes out, you may want to rework your outline so topics flow together more easily. Each heading and subheading (typically taken from your outline) acts as a guidepost for your readers, moving them from one idea to the next.

However, to stay focused during the research and outlining process, you must have a good grasp of your thesis. If you haven't written at least a rough draft of your thesis, now is a perfect time. So, before diving into the writing and revising process, let's look at your thesis in the next chapter.

NOTES

CHAPTER 9

Writing Academic Papers

NOTES

"Either write something worth reading or do something worth writing."

~ BENJAMIN FRANKLIN

Finally. This is the moment you've been waiting for. You've planned. You've researched. You've note taken. You've outlined. And now, you're ready to write! In this chapter, you'll learn how to turn the knowledge in your head into compelling words on a page and craft an academic report from start to finish. You've made it to Step 4: writing and revising.

Step 4: Writing and Revising

But First, the Thesis

If you haven't done so, now is the time to define your thesis. Of course, it can continue to evolve as your ideas develop, but having a working hypothesis will result in a more efficient writing process. In short, your thesis answers a question you pose for the reader. So, let's dive into that concept a little more.

> *Your thesis answers a question you pose for the reader.*

The goal of a thesis statement is to clearly and concisely communicate what your paper is about. In addition, it should help your reader understand the scope and context of your topic and provide a roadmap for the remainder of the work. This means that while the thesis provides an overview of the issue, it may also list important subtopics or categories that provide a framework for the pages that follow.

To write your thesis, you must first determine your topic, then your argument or point (in other words, the "so what?"). Think of your thesis as your paper's "elevator pitch." When I help writers uncover their theses, I often ask them the following seemingly simple questions: "What point are you trying to make? And why should your reader care?" It's surprising how many writers are stumped by these questions. If you *can* answer, however, you're on your way to defining your thesis. If you can respond in a single sentence, you probably already have a working premise.

If you still need more help defining your thesis, start by phrasing your topic as a question, then answer it. Your first attempt probably won't be perfect, and that's okay. You'll have time to refine your thesis as you flesh out the body of your paper.

Remember, your thesis should be located at the beginning of your paper, typically in the first paragraph. It doesn't need to be the opening sentence. You might want to reserve that prime real estate for an especially scintillating "hook."

Start by phrasing your topic as a question, then answer it.

Getting Started

Writing can be a messy, complex process, and there's more than one way to get started. My suggestion is, when you don't know where to begin, just start writing. Below is the approach I use when writing. I've used this process for blog posts, news articles, academic writing, and even this book.

At this point, you have amassed a large amount of information, and you know much more than you think. So, trust yourself and put pen to paper (or fingers to keyboard) with a freewriting session. You can start anywhere you like, but I typically start at the beginning of the piece and conduct a freewriting session for each section, as defined by my outline.

As you're writing, you may realize you need a specific date, fact, or quote that you don't have on hand. That's alright. Make a note or highlight, skip over it for now, and keep on writing. Don't let anything interrupt your flow. Write until you've exhausted your storehouse of knowledge on whatever portion of the paper you selected.

"Writing is Rewriting"

After you've completed your freewriting session for each section of the paper, you'll probably notice

When you don't know where to begin, just start writing.

some gaps. Maybe you need to do additional research, or your outline isn't quite right. These discrepancies are what the rewriting and revising process is all about.

Structured Freewriting

My process for writing and revising generally looks something like this:

1. **Write**

    On Saturday morning, I might tackle a significant portion of my paper or other written work. Remember the elephant analogy? I don't take on the whole project; I mindfully select a specific topic to write about each day. Typically, I spend several hours in a freewriting session. Once the section seems complete (and I feel exhausted), I take a break. But before I power down my laptop, I reread everything I wrote just to make sure it makes sense. I might find a few mistakes here or there, so I do some light editing on that first reread, but usually nothing too drastic. Then I let it sit.

2. **Revise. Then Write.**

    The next day (or the next writing session), I start by reviewing what I wrote last. At this point, I begin to refine and reorganize. Having some mental distance from what I wrote previously gives me the clarity to see mistakes and issues I hadn't seen before. Sure, I'm looking out for significant spelling and grammatical errors, but mostly I'm taking a critical approach to the content. Is it logical? Does the evidence support it? Does it fit with my thesis? Does it flow? But I'm not done yet. This is just my writing session "warm-up." It refreshes my memory on the topic, reminds me where I left off, and primes my brain to write the next portion of the paper.

Note: The better you get at writing, the less time it will take to do this first round of revisions.

Once I've revised the most recently written section, I start drafting the next one. And so on.

3. **Repeat.**

Continue the revise-then-write pattern until you've drafted every major section of your paper. I determine which section to draft next based on my outline. If you're working on a research paper, I recommend aiming for writing sessions that produce about four to six type-written pages, or 1000 to 1600 words. If you have less time to write, compose two pages. If you're experiencing flow and are on a roll, write as many pages as possible.

Data Dump Drafting

An alternative to freewriting is what some call "data dumping." In this approach, you cut and paste ideas from your research notes into your outline. Once you've done so, you'll have a list of bullet points, quotes, and other research notes for each section of your paper. With this method, you'll first organize the notes in each section, then draft content around the data you've collected for each topic, filling in the gaps to create a cohesive essay.

Regardless of which method you use, the outcome is largely the same. In the first approach, you write from memory and then fill in information from your notes after your freewriting session. In the second approach, you start with the supporting data points, quotes, etc., and craft a narrative around them.

I prefer the freewriting method because it forces me to say everything in my own words from the beginning. If you're missing any evidence or need to fact-check later, you absolutely can—and should—do so. No matter which method you choose, however, the goal is simply to get words on the page and start building momentum.

The (Re) Writing Process

By this point, you should have your writing flow established. Here's an example of what your writing sessions might look like. (The topics are examples and will vary depending on the assignment.) Please note that writing sessions do not need to occur on consecutive days, but sometimes it helps if they do.

Session 1: Monday
- Write the Background section

Session 2: Tuesday
- Review and revise the Background
- Write the Historical Context section

Session 3: Friday
- Review and revise the Historical Context
- Write the next section (and so on)

After you've completed your freewriting session, during your revision, you can fill in any research gaps or address any concerns you see. As you review each section, ask yourself if what you wrote ties back to your thesis. If it doesn't, that's probably a good indication it doesn't belong. Next, go back to your outline and ask yourself if the material you just revised might fit better somewhere else. Don't be afraid to remove words, sentences, and even entire paragraphs from your paper—don't get too attached to anything!

Pro Tip: I like to keep a document with "cuts," or deleted information, just in case I decide I need it later. While having this document makes me feel better about cutting things out, I rarely (if ever) put that information back in. Do whatever you need to do to give yourself peace of mind, but don't sacrifice your paper's integrity for unnecessary information simply because you're too attached to let it go.

The Editing Process

Editing comes in multiple varieties: developmental, line editing, SPAG, and more. Think of developmental, or content, revisions as "big picture" restructuring or reorganization. The content revision process is when you decide where and if things belong. Developmental editing also addresses a paper's strengths, weaknesses, logic, and validity of arguments.

Line editing takes a sentence-by-sentence approach and includes a critical look at word choice, phrasing, and sentence structure to produce clear and fluent communication. This type of review also ensures smooth transitions between sentences, paragraphs, and ideas.

SPAG stands for "spelling, punctuation, and grammar" and is a more surface-level editing form. Sometimes referred to as "proofreading," this type of editing focuses on overall "correctness" and avoiding common language errors.

As with your research process, you want to work from big to small when you edit. Therefore, you should review your work for developmental issues to determine whether your logic, organization, and arguments make sense. Next, you should ensure that your claims are accurate and validated and that each section of the paper includes appropriate supporting evidence. Once the report is well organized and supported, you can refine your sentence structure and word choice before proofreading.

NOTES

Writing Right

The best advice I can offer for good writing is to "write right" from the start. Doing so will make the editing process quicker and much more manageable. Secondly, think about organization on every level.

Writing right means practicing good writing hygiene from the moment you put pen to paper. This includes writing in complete sentences and starting your document with correct formatting (font type and size, margins, etc.). Pay attention to word choice and sentence structure, and maintain a consistent voice throughout the piece. Get in the habit of avoiding sentence fragments and incomplete thoughts. The better you write to begin with, the smoother your editing process will go. The more you practice accurate, consistent writing, the easier and faster good writing will become.

In addition, always consider structure as you write. Good organizational structure can make complex concepts easier to understand, but poorly organized writing can stop a reader in their tracks and render the message completely ineffective. Below are some prompts I use to ensure orderly writing from start to finish.

The "Writing Right" Checklist

Paper: First, consider your overall structure (essentially your paper's outline).

- Does every section point back to the thesis?
- Is the order logical, and does it flow?
- Is there anything that doesn't belong?
- Does anything need to be added?

Sections: Second, consider each section's structure.

- Does each section have supporting evidence, citations, and/or quotes?
- If a section consists of multiple parts, or a hierarchy of information, does it present a "roadmap" at the beginning? (For example, if you plan to examine three alternatives to fossil fuels, do you list them upfront before you dive in?)
- Does each section start with a mini-thesis or topic sentence? Scan your paper and ensure it sets forth a clear direction at the beginning of each segment.

Paragraphs: Now, look at each paragraph.
- Does each paragraph have a topic sentence? Depending on the length and style of the paper, I strongly encourage you to consider topic sentences.
- Does each paragraph neatly encompass an idea or related set of ideas?
- Does each paragraph have a clear central idea, supporting details, and a concluding (or transitional) sentence?
- Which paragraphs should be combined to form a single line of thought, and which should be separated or deleted? No single paragraph should cover too much material or change topics in the middle.

Sentences: You'll do a sentence-by-sentence review in the final stages of editing and proofreading your paper. However, below are some items to look out for, in addition to SPAG.
- Add transitional words and phrases between sentences, paragraphs, and sections.
- Check for fragments and run-on sentences.

- Turn complex sentences into shorter, simpler sentences.
- Double-check the definitions of any words you aren't absolutely sure of the meaning.
- Remove any jargon or clichés from your writing. Replace them with direct, simple, and descriptive language.

Step 5: Finishing Touches

The final step in the writing process typically involves the following:

- Introduction/Conclusion
- In-text Citations and References
- Appendices
- Formatting
- Proofreading
- Feedback

Introduction and Conclusion. To begin the finishing touches of your paper, you may want to rework your paper's introduction and conclusion. The reason I recommend writers wait until the end of a report to finalize these sections is that up until that point, they are typically still collecting data and forming the final analysis. If you write the introduction before you complete the body of the paper, it is likely to be incomplete, inaccurate, or both. The same idea holds true for the conclusion. Wait until your report is fully baked before identifying and summarizing the main ideas. That way, you'll know the paper precisely follows the introduction, and the conclusion impeccably flows from the paper.

References. Next, review all in-text citations and reference pages. Ensure you appropriately cite every data point, statistic, quote, or idea you borrowed from someone else in the text (through parenthetical, numeric, or notated citations) and in a bibliography or references section, depending on the style guide your instructor selected.

Pro Tip: For help citing many different genres of work, try the Purdue Online Writing Lab's (OWL) Citation Generator tool.[17]

Appendices. If you haven't done so already, add any graphs, charts, or tables referenced in the paper's body to the appendix. Review the titles of any figures in the appendix to ensure they match what's listed in the report. For example, if you write "See Figure 5 in the appendix," make sure it's labeled that way and none of your labels conflict or overlap.

Formatting. Formatting is your friend **IF** you use it correctly. Review your entire paper to ensure the pages are set up according to your professor's guidelines, including font styles and sizes, margins, and line spacing. No matter which style guide your instructor prefers (MLA, APA, Chicago, etc.), be sure your style is consistent! For example, if you use the Oxford comma once, use it EVERY SINGLE TIME.

Proofreading. At this point in the process, you should have dealt with any structural issues, so you can focus on refining your report's language. You probably fixed most of the obvious SPAG (spelling, punctuation, and grammar) errors during the revision process, but now it's time to perfect your writing. First, I suggest reading the paper from start to finish, preferably aloud. I also find it helpful to read the work multiple times, looking for different types of errors with each pass. For example, I may focus on clarity and brevity in one read, then style and formatting in the next, and finally, flow and transitions. You should proofread the final version of your paper a *minimum* of three times before submitting it.

NOTES

Once I've refined my work as much as possible, I'll run it through Grammarly to catch any errors I missed. With tools like Grammarly, Hemingway, and citation generators, you have no excuse to turn in an unpolished (or un-proofed) paper.

Pro Tip: If you've read your paper so many times you can't see straight, try reading it backward instead. That's right, backward. Novelty often shocks our brains into greater clarity and focus. (Think of it as a slap across the face for your brain.) So don't be surprised when you find mistakes using this method you would have otherwise missed.

Feedback. Last but not least, always seek feedback on your writing. I like to think of myself as a decent (perhaps even accomplished) writer, but that doesn't stop me from seeking input from others. Depending on the type of paper you're writing, you may wish to get feedback from friends, family, peers, or industry experts. Just be sure to give your reviewers enough time to respond with their insights and yourself enough time to implement them. Remember, once you receive feedback, you've got more work to do. You'll want to consider your reviewers' comments thoughtfully and revise your paper accordingly. Pay particular attention to any themes repeated by multiple readers. If two or more reviewers offer the same feedback, you'd be wise to revise.

I hope you've benefited from this brief writing tutorial and learned ways to improve your academic writing skills. I encourage you to master the writing tips in the next chapter, and please don't forget to review Appendix A for more writing resources.

10 Tips for Better Writing

"The most valuable of all talents is that of never using two words when one will do."
~ THOMAS JEFFERSON

I've read many books on writing, most of which put me straight to sleep. So rather than lecture you on subject-verb agreement and split infinitives, I'll simply share my top 10 tips for writing well. These powerful pointers will take your writing from average to *"A"* level in no time.

1. Focus on clarity and brevity.

The best way to showcase your knowledge is by writing in a way that's easy to read and understand, so focus on making each sentence clear and concise. When my writing lacks clarity, I ask myself, "What am I really trying to say?" Then I write the answer down. Remove any superfluous language (or "fluff"). Rather than saying something twice in a different way, say it once clearly and emphatically.

2. Use the active, rather than passive, voice.

Doing so improves tone and creates greater clarity by eliminating unnecessary words.

Incorrect: My first visit to Malibu will always be remembered by me.
Correct: I will always remember my first visit to Malibu.

3. Make statements positive.

Even a *negative* should be expressed in *positive* form.

Incorrect: He wasn't on time very much.
Correct: He usually arrived late.

Incorrect: not honest
Correct: dishonest

4. Use specific, concrete language.

In other words, don't be vague.

Incorrect: He engaged in bad behavior for a long time.
Correct: He harassed his coworkers every day for a year.

5. Avoid clichés, slang, and jargon. Opt for vivid, precise, and descriptive language instead.

Common clichés include phrases such as "rule of thumb," "can of worms," and "think outside the box." The problem with these overused expressions is that they demonstrate a lack of original thought and creativity,

NOTES

and their initial reference is often irrelevant. The same is true for slang, which can quickly become outdated or may translate poorly to different geographic, social, or demographic groups.

Jargon is language specific to a group or profession and is often found in technical, bureaucratic, and business writing. Jargon includes overly technical terminology and acronyms (especially those without definitions).

Instead of clichés, slang, or jargon, aim to write in a way anyone can understand, even without background knowledge of the subject. The best way to do this is to express your ideas using fresh, creative language that evokes vivid imagery in your reader's mind. When you spot a cliché in your writing, replace it with an analogy or description all your own.

6. Remove the word "that."

Remember what I said about being clear and concise? In most instances (I'd say 9 out of 10), you can remove the word "that" to make your sentence more succinct without compromising the message.

7. Simplify: Write short sentences. Use simple words.

The easiest way to make your writing more clear and less prone to grammatical errors is to write short sentences. Not only are complex sentences difficult to read, but they are also more inclined to suffer from structural issues such as subject-verb agreement. By splitting a compound sentence into two, you can communicate in a more effective, less error-prone way.

Whenever you can, use the simplest language to make your point. For example, write "use" rather than "utilize."

8. Delete ~~too many~~ needless words.

See what I did there? Below is a list of phrases that can almost always be removed:

- "due to the fact"
- "in order to"
- "the fact that"
- "who is"
- "which was"

The following are some helpful substitutions for superfluous phrases.

- "Due to the fact" → because
- "In the event of" → if
- "In regard to" → regarding
- "The question as to whether" → whether
- "A lot of" → many
- "On an annual basis" → yearly
- "She is a woman who" → she

9. Watch out for misplaced modifiers.

A misplaced modifier is a word (or group of words) that is improperly separated from the word it describes. Below are a few examples.

Incorrect: *"My daughter ate a cold bowl of cereal for breakfast."*
Correct: "My daughter ate a bowl of cold cereal for breakfast."

Incorrect: *"On my way home, I found a gold woman's watch."*

Correct: "On my way home, I found a woman's gold watch."

10. Use style and formatting to communicate your message.

You may *think* the **font** you USE and your style and *formatting* doesn't matter.

But the truth is, your formatting can either support or detract from your message.

Use bold typeface, bullet points, headings, subheadings, italics, etc., to emphasize key messages. This will help your reader easily locate the main ideas and follow a logical and orderly progression through a hierarchy of information.

Part III

The Busy Student's Guide
to
Life

CHAPTER 11

Everything Else

"People who want to appear clever rely on memory. People who want to get things done make lists."

~ PETER MCWILLIAMS

How do you deal with everything outside of school that you need to manage? The short answer? Make lists.

But we can't end the chapter there, so let's further explore this unbelievably simple tool on which the best productivity experts rely.

The Secret to Project Management

The best tip I learned to manage my work, my life, *and* my business came from a design student. As my classmates and I marveled at our fellow designer's impeccable project management skills, we asked her to share her secret. "Make lists," she said. "I find myself constantly making lists, so I don't forget anything." This tiny tip took my management skills from mediocre to unmatched. Here's why.

According to David Allen, author of *Getting Things Done*,[18] the secret to eliminating cognitive clutter is to move every unfinished task or project from your brain and capture it somewhere else. When we capture and close these "open loops," we create more mental space and clarity, which allows our minds to focus on the task at hand, making our time more effective. For this reason, list-making is essential to the success of any busy person. I know I can't possibly remember everything, so instead, I write it all down.

Make Multiple Lists

Create separate lists for everything you need to do in your personal, professional, and academic life. The goal is to get everything cluttering your mind out of your head and onto a notepad, so you can think in a clear and focused way. I maintain either hard copy or electronic lists for virtually everything: errands, schoolwork, groceries, etc., and I keep each list in the place I intend to use it. This practice supports another time management technique I love: batching. Batching simply means grouping similar tasks together so you spend less time switching between tasks, burning up valuable cognitive energy.

For example, at work, I have a physical notepad on my desk with my list of priorities for the day and the week. I also use an online notepad to house my long- and medium-term work projects, so I don't forget about them while focusing on my daily tasks. This list lives in the cloud so that when I remember something important (even at 2 a.m.), I can add it no matter where I am.

Batching: grouping similar tasks together so you spend less time and mental energy switching between activities.

I also keep electronic lists for each person and department I meet with regularly. For example, I have a separate digital notepad list for the following: Supervisor, Assistant, Chief of Staff, Marketing Director, Events Team, and so on. Here, I keep agenda items for the next meeting, so I don't forget any projects, tasks, or follow-up conversations.

In my vehicle, I typically keep a notepad with a list of places I need to go and errands I need to run. I see it as soon as I get into my car without needing to access any digital devices. This is one of the few paper lists I still maintain because it helps me resist the urge to check the to-do list on my mobile phone while driving. The list in my car might read: "Drop off at dry cleaners; get car washed; pick up groceries," for example.

I maintain my grocery list on the notepad on my mobile device, so I always have it with me when I'm roaming the supermarket aisles. I've left far too many handwritten grocery lists at home, so now I always save this list to the cloud.

Last, I usually keep my academic "to-do" list wherever I store my syllabus and other class materials. I typically use the "weekly assignments" section of the syllabus as my default task list and make any notes I need in the margins. Each week, I highlight assignments in the syllabus to which I want to pay special attention, and I mark off everything I've already done, such as each chapter or article I've read. This process helps me keep track of my work and dive into my study sessions without wasting time deciphering where I left off.

The following images are examples of lists I maintain regularly. Still, I want to emphasize that no matter where or how you compose your lists, the goal is to get open loops out of your head and recorded somewhere else. So, for example, in the same way you might clear your desk of clutter before starting a big project, you also want to clear your mind before opening a textbook to study.

NOTES

Sample "To-Do" Lists

Today's Priorities

call doctor to reschedule
send new client proposal
stop by grocery store

This Week's Priorities

follow up on outstanding
   proposals
pay phone bill
complete copy edit of book

Errands

stop by library
pick up dry cleaning
put air in tire
get nails done

Calls

dermatologist
insurance agent
return Meghan's call
catch up with Scott

Emails

contact vendor for tracking
   number
send weekly summary to
   Client A
follow up with Client B
send proposal to Client C

Grocery List

eggs
coconut milk
salmon
bananas
blueberries
avocados
spinach

Discipline Trumps Talent

When I was in fifth grade, it occurred to me that the world holds so many interesting and exciting things to do, learn, and become that I'd never be able to accomplish them all...

UNLESS I learned to manage my time. If I could make every minute count, I could do more than my peers, who wasted the same amount of time I put to work. So that night, I wrote out my ideal after-school schedule on a sheet of lined notebook paper. It included all the activities I had to do (homework, practicing piano, eating dinner, etc.) and the activities I wanted to do (watch my favorite shows, talk to my best friend on the phone, read for fun). I then presented my plan to the chief executives in my life at the time, my parents. Despite the stringent house rule prohibiting television before homework, Mom and Dad approved. Thanks to my handwritten schedule, which was essentially a contract between the executive team and me, they could see that studying had a dedicated time and place. Consequently, I was free to operate on a timeline that worked for me.

Looking back, what might seem like a silly childhood story was the beginning of a habit that has transformed my life, my work, and my ability to get things done. Did the scheduling habit I started at age ten pay off the way I hoped it would at that time? I think so. Because of my ability to plan, organize, and manage time, I've obtained two master's degrees, had multiple careers across industries, worked as a U.S. diplomat overseas, written a novel, earned several certifications, traveled extensively, and started my own business. However, I don't attribute my accomplishments to intelligence or even hard work. Instead, I attribute them to discipline. I learned the discipline of doing difficult things as a child, like tinkering away at piano keys even—and especially—when I didn't want to. I demonstrated that same sensibility when I structured my own after-school hours and then stuck to my plan.

The problem with adulthood is that no one will "ground" you if you don't do what you're supposed to do. Therefore, you need to develop the discipline to consistently execute the following behaviors:

Daily Disciplines for Productivity

1. **Gather and organize** what needs to be accomplished. Lists help tremendously.
2. **Follow a system** (schedule, routine, plan, etc.) that supports the completion of the projects and tasks you've identified.
3. **Batch similar tasks together** for greater efficiency. For example, spend a specific amount of time reading and responding to email each day rather than checking your inbox all day.
4. **Have the strength to say no** (mainly to yourself) if you're falling behind on your work.

The wonderful thing about planning and scheduling is it's easy to see if you haven't met your objectives. If your weekly to-do list hasn't been touched, or if you've missed a scheduled study session, the onus is on you to take action, which may mean waking up earlier for the rest of the week or saying no to a last-minute dinner invitation. "Grounding" yourself is a hallmark of discipline because it shows you have the courage to say no, even to yourself.

> *Discipline is the desire to fiercely honor your commitments—to yourself and others—and to show up each day with integrity and consistency.*

Discipline is the desire to fiercely honor your commitments—to yourself and others—and to show up each day with integrity and consistency. Discipline also means having the strength to get back up when you fall, learn from your mistakes, and recognize that even when you miss the mark, tomorrow is a new day. Discipline isn't about perfection; instead, it's the patience to work *through* your imperfections. Over time, this relentless dedication breeds excellence and inspires trust.

The Power of Routine

You've probably heard the statistic that humans make about 35,000 decisions per day. I don't know if that number is accurate for everyone, but my guess is you make more daily decisions than you realize, and each decision, however mundane, requires energy and, therefore, willpower. As discussed earlier, a simple way to short-circuit decision making is to turn activities into habits. When your routines are automatic, you don't lose energy deciding what to do or when and how to do it. Instead, you create more mental space for the things that count. So, whether you habitually turn on the kettle the moment you get out of bed or immediately lace up your running shoes, the more essential activities and positive habits you make automatic, the more willpower and decision-making capacity you'll have for other things.

This is why a dedicated study schedule is *literally* a "no-brainer." It eliminates the time and effort you would otherwise spend:

1. Organizing your study schedule anew each week.
2. Renegotiating that time if something came up.
3. Fighting with your inner child (who would probably always rather goof off) every time you open a textbook.

When you have a lot on your plate, creating automatic routines and closing open loops by capturing information on lists can reduce your cognitive load enough to improve your performance—or at least prevent you from blowing a fuse!

The Weekly Roundup

I like to do a weekly roundup to synthesize my list-making and scheduling activities, which go hand-in-hand. Ideally, this process occurs just before the start of the week (either Sunday afternoon or early Monday morning). During this time, I write to-do lists for everything I need to accomplish personally and professionally that week. Then, I review my calendar(s) for any significant meetings, deadlines, or special events. Once I've checked my task lists and available time, I start scheduling key activities, which might include planning extra time to prepare for an upcoming meeting or scheduling my workouts for the week. During this roundup session, I also review any remaining to-do items from the previous week, which helps me harness unfinished business, so I don't have surprises later on (like an arrest warrant for an unpaid parking ticket that slipped through the cracks).

The weekly roundup's primary objective is to prevent things from sneaking up on you. Perhaps you've had the experience of walking into your office on Monday morning to an avalanche of phone calls, emails, meetings, and emergencies. When that happens, you often find that by the time you're finally able to catch your breath and take a moment to write your to-do list, it's already Friday. You can avoid this scenario by being proactive. When you take control of your week through regular roundup sessions, the "Sunday scaries" will subside, and you might even be excited to start a new week.

The "Next Step" Method

What happens when a problem is so complex you don't know where to begin or how to break it down? Or what if you're simply too exhausted or overwhelmed by your "to-do" list to create a plan? In those moments (and trust me, they happen), you need a method to help you do *something* ... anything! Following is the process I use to kick-start a stalled effort.

> ### The "Next Step" Method
> **Do one thing, right now, that gets you a step closer to your goal.**
> *Pro Tip: The best next step usually takes less than five minutes.*

I call it the "next step" principle, and I start by asking myself one simple question: What's the next step I can take, no matter how small, to get a little closer to my goal? For a perfectionist like me, having this type of backup plan for complex issues is a lifesaver. Most of the time, the next step takes less than five minutes. It can be a short email, a text message, or a quick internet search.

For example, let's say an issue with a friend or family member is weighing on your mind. You might not be able to solve the entire problem in a day, but you can send a voice note with a kind word or reach out to schedule a lunch date. Or maybe you have an elephant-sized research paper hanging over your head, and you're procrastinating because you just don't know where to begin. Before you go to bed, read the assignment once through and brainstorm three potential topic ideas. That's it. Neither of these first steps results in a final solution or finished product, but they start the elephant-eating process, and sometimes that first "bite" is the biggest, psychologically speaking!

At least that's true for me. For example, when I set out to write this book, I dutifully listed it on my to-do list week after week, and I'm embarrassed to admit that for months it sat on my list untouched. Then, one day I came to terms with the truth—I was procrastinating. The reason I was procrastinating is that writing a book is a big, hairy, audacious, and super scary goal, and I wasn't sure how or where to begin. However, I also knew if I let my fears and muddled mind get the best of me, I'd never get started.

That day, I had about an hour of free time, so I set my excuses aside and did something I knew I could accomplish that afternoon: I wrote the introduction to this book. Because I didn't need extensive research or even an outline to do it, I started with a freewriting session and let the words come from my heart. Over subsequent weeks, I refined and revised that initial draft, but I found that simply beginning the writing process opened the floodgates. Once I started, I couldn't stop. One hour of writing that day turned into eight hours of writing the next day, and the next, and the next. Within a mere matter of weeks, I had a workable draft.

I share this story to remind you that no one executes all the principles in this book perfectly, including me. Personal effectiveness is a lifelong commitment to working through your fears and doing the "hard things" in life, even—and especially—when you don't want to do them. The more you put this book's principles into practice, the easier they will become. The sooner you execute the first action for a big project or challenging problem, the more quickly subsequent steps reveal themselves. Never forget that being a learner means always being a work in progress, and that growth is the joy of learning.

> ***Never forget that being a learner means always being a work in progress, and that growth is the joy of learning.***

CHAPTER 12

Biohacking for Scholars

"Think in the morning. Act in the noon.
Eat in the evening. Sleep in the night."

~ WILLIAM BLAKE

In the past several chapters, you've mastered study skills and habits that will amplify your learning. Now, I want to introduce you to the latest science that can take your focus and concentration to the next level. However, no biohack is truly effective unless it's executed alongside a foundation of good health. So, let's begin by reviewing the basics.

Laying the Foundation

A healthy mental, physical, and emotional state begins with proper sleep, nutrition, and exercise. You cannot expect to perform at your peak without these essential building blocks, so let's take a deeper look at them, as well as at some other healthy habits you should incorporate daily.

Sleep

While I don't consider sleep a "hack," the quality and quantity of your sleep are vitally important to your well-being. Consider it the base upon which the following tools build. Studies show a parabolic relationship[19] between sleep and cognitive function, meaning both too little and too much sleep can make you mentally sluggish. According to research, the ideal amount of sleep is seven to nine hours a night for young adults and seven to eight hours for older adults.[20] Additionally, a chronic lack of sleep can seriously impair cognitive function, as can a sleepless all-nighter. This impairment affects judgment and decision making, which is why getting enough sleep before an exam is imperative.

Movement

According to Dr. Sanjay Gupta, physical exertion is the only scientifically documented way to improve brain health and function.[21] You should also note that exercise and movement are two different things, and your body needs both. According to Dr. Gupta, movement can improve brain power by helping to increase, repair, and maintain brain cells, making you more productive and alert throughout the day.

Movement supports brain health by releasing a brain-derived neurotrophic factor (BDNF). This protein not only promotes the creation of new brain cells (neurogenesis), but it also protects existing neurons and helps them connect and communicate with each other. The best part is that research suggests moderate, rather than intense, activity is ideal for brain function,[22] which means even a brisk walk can help you think better!

Sunlight

Another healthy habit to layer on top of good sleep and regular exercise includes safe exposure to sunlight, especially when you rise, and avoiding UVB light exposure at night. Just five to ten minutes outside on a sunny morning will do the trick. To maximize the bio benefits, don't wear sunglasses or view sunlight through a window or windshield. Sunlight has been scientifically proven to increase energy, maximize alertness, and improve mood and focus,[23] but do you really need someone to tell you that sunlight is awesome? Just remember to wear sunblock and protective clothing, and please don't look directly at the sun.

In the evening, avoid artificial light from computers and other digital devices between the hours of 10 p.m. and 4 a.m. Doing so will reinforce your natural circadian rhythms and support a healthy sleep cycle. Keep in mind that chronic late-night light exposure suppresses dopamine, which can impede learning.[24] If you must use your computer after 10 p.m., consider blue-blocking lenses or screens and lower the brightness level of your device.

Nutrition

We'll learn about "brain foods" in the next section, but before we do, I want to stress the importance of nutrition. Food fuels our bodies and minds, so if you're going to operate at your best, start by eating a balanced, healthy diet and staying well hydrated. Avoid excess sugar, salt, and processed foods, and opt for minimally processed, natural, whole foods.

When I decide what to eat, I ask myself how far removed that food is from the ingredients it's made of. For example, a banana is on one end of the spectrum, and a Twinkie is on the other. Whenever possible, seek organic sources of plant or animal protein and "raw" fruits, vegetables, nuts, and seeds. (Uncooked, unheated, and unpasteurized fruits and vegetables, including cold-pressed juices and raw nut- and seed-based foods, deliver more nutrients and live enzymes

NOTES

than cooked or processed versions of the same.) These natural foods should form the base of your diet. Then, if you want to optimize your nutrition for even better cognition, sprinkle in the "brain foods" mentioned below, but always start with a healthy baseline diet.

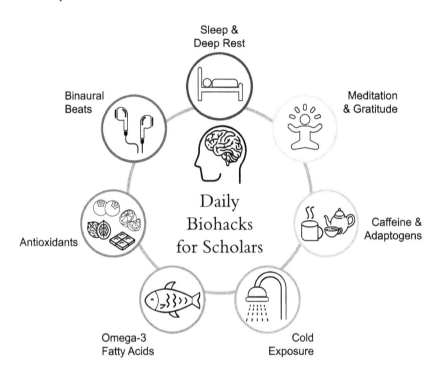

Caffeine, Adaptogens, and Superfood Lattes

While caffeine has several brain benefits, such as increased alertness, improved mood, and sharpened concentration, I encourage you to amp up your average cup of joe by opting for one of the following superfood lattes to maximize brain benefits. These coffee substitutes contain a combination of powerful antioxidants and adaptogens. Simply put, adaptogens help your body respond to stress and fatigue. No matter where you get your caffeine, though, aim for 100–400 milligrams daily,[25] ideally in the morning, so you don't disrupt your sleep routine.

Matcha

I was a fan of matcha long before it was trendy. You can read about why I call it the "super tea" in an article I wrote for *The Huffington Post*, which you can find in the Recommended Reading section at the end of this book. The reason I love this superfood so much is that it contains L-theanine, which calms the body, and, when paired with the caffeine in matcha, sharpens the mind.[26] L-theanine has been shown to reduce stress and anxiety and may also increase concentration.

Golden Milk

This superfood recipe contains two brain-boosting ingredients. Ashwagandha is an Indian herb used in traditional Ayurvedic medicine and is said to improve memory, cognition, and possibly even attention span. Often classified as an adaptogen, ashwagandha is also known for relieving stress and anxiety. What's more, turmeric (the spice that gives golden milk its bright yellow color) is a powerful antioxidant. Curcumin, the active ingredient in turmeric, can cross the blood-brain barrier, meaning it can directly enter the brain and benefit cells there.[27] Some of those benefits may include improving memory, boosting mood, and helping brain cells grow.

Mushroom "Coffee"

Lion's mane mushrooms contain bioactive substances that beneficially affect the body and brain. Studies have found that lion's mane contains compounds that can stimulate brain cell growth and repair. (Did you catch that?) In addition, research indicates that the mushroom's anti-inflammatory properties can reduce symptoms of anxiety and boost the immune system.[28]

In ancient Chinese medicine, reishi mushrooms have long been associated with increased memory. Modern science shows reishi also boosts the immune system and reduces fatigue.[29]

"Bulletproof" Coffee

Dave Asprey, self-proclaimed biohacker and creator of Bulletproof Coffee, is known for his brain-boosting java, which includes grass-fed butter (or ghee) and MCT (coconut) oil.[30] This supercharged combination provides essential nutrients, such as omega-3 fatty acids and antioxidants, as well as brain-fueling ketones. Medium-chain triglyceride, or MCT, fatty acids occur naturally in coconuts and, because of their molecular structure, can easily cross the blood-brain barrier, providing instant energy to the brain—in other words, brain power! What's more, MCT oil is shown to improve long-term memory and executive cognitive function,[31] so why not give your coffee *and* your brain a boost with MCTs? (You can also add MCT oil to any hot beverage or smoothie.)

Note: The quality of nutritional supplements varies. Always speak with your healthcare provider before adding supplements to your diet.

Omega-3 Fatty Acids

Omega-3 fatty acids are essential for brain health and function.[32] Did you know that the majority of your brain is composed of fat, and most of that fat is in the form of omega-3 fatty acids? Omega-3s are the brain's building blocks; they build brain and nerve cells, support memory, and even help regulate emotion.[33]

You can find omega-3s in fish, vegetable oils, walnuts, flaxseed, chia seeds, leafy vegetables, and of course, supplements.[34] But no matter the source, aim for one to three grams of EPA omega-3 fatty acids per day.[35]

Brain-Friendly Snacks

You might be happy to hear that dark chocolate, nuts, and fruit are some of the best brain foods for scholars. Let's look at these staples, plus a few more.

Chocolate

Dark chocolate and cocoa powder are filled with brain-boosting flavonoids, caffeine, and antioxidants. Flavonoids are bioactive compounds with antioxidant properties, and the flavonoids in chocolate are thought to enhance learning and memory.[36]

Nuts

Because nuts are a source of healthy fat, antioxidants, and vitamin E, they have a positive effect on brain health by protecting cells against free-radical damage. While almonds are said to improve memory,[37] walnuts may be the most beneficial for your brain because, in addition to the attributes above, they also deliver those omega-3s we discussed earlier.[38]

Eggs

Eggs may also boost the brain because they are high in nutrients such as folate and choline, which are linked to improved mood, memory, and mental function.[39] Eggs are also a high-quality source of protein, fat, and two antioxidants (lutein and zeaxanthin) known to protect the eyes from degeneration and harmful sunlight.[40]

Berries

The pigments (anthocyanins) in deeply hued fruits like blueberries, blackberries, raspberries, and strawberries can cross the blood-brain barrier, resulting in powerful protection and brain-enhancing benefits. Not only do berries contain flavonoids, which have been shown to improve memory, but they also contain potent antioxidants that fight oxidative stress and inflammation. A study conducted with young and old participants found that those who consumed blueberries showed increased blood flow to the brain and improved memory and attention.[41] Blueberries, in particular, are thought to aid the communication between brain cells, helping to improve memory and cognitive processes.[42]

Citrus Fruit

Similarly, oranges are also high in antioxidants that help fight free radical damage to brain cells. Additionally, citrus fruits are known to promote stress relief, largely because vitamin C allows the body to process cortisol more quickly. For this reason, oranges make an excellent pre-exam or pre-presentation snack. Furthermore, vitamin C is also shown to improve focus, memory, attention, and decision speed.[43]

Binaural Beats

Binaural beats can help prime your mind for focus. Binaural beats are sound waves with two slightly different frequencies that, when heard together, create the perception of a third sound frequency. (Think of it as an auditory illusion.) Binaural beats are most effective when you listen to them with headphones or earbuds a few minutes before starting a work session.

Studies show that binaural beats increase working memory by helping the brain organize and retain the information you absorb throughout the day.[44] At lower frequencies, they've been linked to relaxation, reduced anxiety, positivity, and meditative and creative states. Binaural beats ranging from 14–40 Hz have been linked to improved concentration, problem solving, memory, and learning.[45]

You can access binaural beats for free on YouTube, Spotify, and other apps. You can also find a link in the Online Resources section of my website if you'd like to give this brain-boosting soundtrack a try.

While binaural beats can be effective *before* a working session, white, pink, or brown noise may be helpful *during* focused study sessions. Personally, I like to work in silence or with noise-canceling headphones or earplugs when I can't control the sounds in my environment.

Cold Therapy

Cold exposure is known to increase dopamine, epinephrine, and cortisol and thus improve focus, concentration, and even mood.[46] While I occasionally engage in cryotherapy, I'm personally not a fan of ice baths. However, you don't need extreme experiences to reap the benefits of cold therapy. Even a one- to five-minute cold shower before or after a study session can help solidify learning.

Meditation

As mentioned before, meditation can improve focus and reduce anxiety, which can be especially helpful if you suffer from exam jitters. Not only does meditation lower blood pressure, but it can also improve creativity, intuition, and self-awareness.[47] I recommend starting with a two- to five-minute meditation a day in the morning and working up from there. As a busy student, if you can squeeze in two five-minute meditation sessions, one in the morning before you start your day and one in the evening before studying, you'll build the mental muscles you need for better focus and attention.

NOTES

Gratitude

I know I've mentioned this practice before, but gratitude affects the brain so profoundly it bears repeating.[48] Gratitude can boost serotonin, which in turn activates the production of dopamine (the "feel good" hormone). So, not only do positive thoughts make you feel happier, the dopamine they produce also helps you stay focused and motivated.[49] According to Stanford neuroscientist Andrew Huberman, dopamine "puts you back in the fight and allows you to fight longer and further. If you look at high performers ... they have gratitude practices, and they incorporate them."[50]

The Beginner's Guide to Gratitude & Meditation

While there are many ways to exercise gratitude, I like to incorporate my gratitude practice into my daily meditation and breathwork. If you're new to any of these practices, use this as a guide to get started.

- After tuning out all distractions, start with deep diaphragmatic breathing to calm the nervous system.
- Then, set a timer (try using the Calm app's "Timed Meditation" feature) and sit in silence or with ambient nature sounds. Continue breathing and consciously let go of any negative feelings or thoughts.
- Don't try to rush through a numbered gratitude list. Instead, once your mind is clear and your body is calm, envision the people, things, and truths you're grateful for. Then sit with them for a while, soaking up all the joy, peace, and positivity they bring.
- Once in a positive mindset, try not to think consciously. Instead, listen without judgement.

This practice is one I've developed over time, and based on my research, this combination of deep breathing, meditation, and visualization is a powerful way to change your mental state. However, I encourage you to experiment and find the best approach for you.

Science tells us that gratitude puts the mind in an alpha state, which can make you feel calm, increase creativity, and help you learn new things. But I prefer to think of gratitude as *magic*. Words can't explain the calmness and clarity true gratitude brings, so I highly recommend you experience it for yourself.

NOTES

Deliberate Drishti

Drishti is the Sanskrit word for "gaze" or "focal point." If you'd like to take your meditation a step further, I suggest focusing your eyes on a single location. While it may be easier to avoid distraction by meditating with closed eyes, focusing your eye muscles on a physical object (not a digital one like a cell phone or computer screen) can help prime your brain for focused work.[51]

Think back to the speed-reading technique we learned in Chapter 5 to help focus your eyes on the page. In that instance, focusing the eyes was a precursor to concentration and reading comprehension. Similarly, a focused mind follows a focused gaze, so practicing your "drishti" for at least 30 seconds and up to three minutes before studying can help. And don't forget to blink!

Deliberate visual focus is much harder than it sounds, which is why I recommend stacking it on top of an existing habit such as meditation. Alternatively, you might want to spend a few minutes working on your drishti while listening to binaural beats before a study session. Test these techniques in small daily doses and see what works best for you.

Power Naps

I love a good nap, and after reading about the brain benefits of napping, you will too! Naps not only improve cognitive performance and reduce fatigue, but according to a University of Berkeley study, afternoon naps boost the brain's capacity to learn. The study shows that naps essentially clear out the brain's short-term memory storage to make room for new information. According to assistant professor and lead researcher Matthew Walker, "Sleep not only rights the wrong of prolonged wakefulness, but at a neurocognitive level, it moves you beyond where you were before you took a nap."[52]

Now that you know naps improve cognitive performance, aid short-term memory, and help you learn and retain information, I hope you'll doze more often. If you want to take your naps to the next level, try pairing them with a cup of joe. One study showed that ingesting 200 milligrams of caffeine (or the equivalent of a grande-sized coffee) and then taking a 10- to 20-minute power nap will not only prevent you from oversleeping, but it will help you get the most out of your nap.[53] You'll wake up alert and ready to focus.

Yoga Nidra

Finally, you may experience times when you're exhausted and can't sleep, yet you must press on with your tasks. These moments are when nonsleep deep rest, or yoga nidra, is a lifesaver. You may have experienced yoga nidra during a guided meditation in a yoga class. However, yoga nidra, or yogic sleep, is different from most meditation practices, which are performed seated. Not only is yoga nidra performed lying down, it takes your brain a step beyond the theta (or meditative) state to delta, the state associated with the deepest sleep and restoration.[54] This state of deep relaxation is not only rejuvenating to the body, but it also sharpens the mind.

As a recovering insomniac, practicing yoga nidra taught me that even when you can't sleep, your body can still benefit from deep rest. For me, my overactive mind is typically what keeps my body from retiring. Yoga nidra helps quiet the mind while rejuvenating the body. (Refer to the Online Resources on my website, https://www.get-the-degree.com/blog/get-the-degree-online-resources, for links to yoga nidra videos.) Another activity that helps me get into a state of nonsleep deep rest is sound bathing. I now consider sound baths a part of my regular health and wellness routine and attend these soothing sound sessions at least once a week.

"On the Go" Hacks

Below are a couple of hacks I use when I'm exhausted but need to persist. Neither requires a lot of space, time, or special equipment, and you can do them at home, at school, or in the office.

Mini Cold Therapy

If you can't take a cold shower, try splashing cold water on your face instead. Consider this a miniature form of cold therapy that will wake up your senses and refresh your mind.

Office Yoga

Another helpful hack I use when I'm fatigued is a quick stretching session. I find heart-opening backbending postures the most invigorating, and they can release much of the tension created by the repetitive "rounded" postures we tend to assume when studying. Spinal twists are also great for relieving the stress caused by sitting. Search "office yoga" for video tutorials or refer to the Online Resources on my website for a five-minute office yoga video link.

The Biohacking Buffet

While I don't expect you to incorporate all of these hacks into your daily routine, you may discover significant benefits from adding a few to your weekly schedule. So, give them a try and decide which ones work best for you. You can also leverage them when you need a little extra learning boost. You might be surprised at how healthy habits like good sleep and nutrition can transform your well-being and cognitive performance.

CHAPTER 13

Career Development

"I've always believed that if you put in the work, the results will come."

~ MICHAEL JORDAN

I'll be the first to admit I'm not an expert on career development, but I do know a thing or two about getting a dream job.

When I was in sixth grade, I decided I wanted to be a diplomat (even though I wasn't sure exactly what that meant at the time). About 13 years later, I was formally sworn in by the U.S. Secretary of State as a Foreign Service Officer and Diplomat for the U.S. Government.

I also dreamed of owning my own business before I turned 30, so after a significant career change, I studied the process and officially launched my company at age 29. Later in life, I was hellbent on becoming a consultant, and not just any consultant. I had my heart set on a "Big Four" firm with a longstanding international reputation. After many months of preparation and interviews, I finally landed my third dream job.

I've had many career twists and turns along the way. Sometimes, I felt like my career was regressing rather than progressing. Still, over time I've learned that even the "building" years yield valuable insights and skills that are usually imperative later on. Let me offer a few examples from my own experience.

- As a writer, editor, and journalist I learned the art of professional communication and developed a deep appreciation for the duty and responsibility of the Fourth Estate.
- As a Foreign Service Officer, I learned the skills of tact, diplomacy, and how to say "no" in a way that honored others' dignity. I also learned to represent something greater than myself.
- As a classroom lecturer and an adjunct faculty member, I learned the nuanced art of public speaking: how to speak extemporaneously, read a room, and think on my feet.
- As a marketer, I honed my sales and communication skills.
- As a designer, I learned everything I needed to know about client service and project management.
- As a leader and senior manager, I combined all of the above skills to drive strategic initiatives forward by building high-performing teams and sustainable systems that withstand the pressure of a scaling business.
- And now, as a consultant, I help other leaders and organizations do the same.

As an author, I'm still learning, but I hope you'll allow me to share a few tips I've used to build and develop my career over the past decades.

Uncover Your Strengths

The best place to start your job search is with a strengths inventory. Many career development centers offer assessments for free; I encourage you to take advantage of that service. One of my favorite inventories is *StrengthsFinder 2.0*. (More on this resource in the next chapter.) Remember, a strength isn't just something you're good at. It's also something you enjoy.

> *Remember, a strength isn't just something you're good at. It's also something you enjoy.*

Your strengths energize and enliven you. For me, they include writing, teaching, and communicating in various ways. Discover yours by answering the following questions.

FINDING CAREER DIRECTION

These questions will help you uncover career paths that build upon your strengths and give you a sense of purpose. Take a moment to answer the following questions.

1. **What do I enjoy doing?**

2. **What am I good at? What do others think I'm good at?**

3. **Where can I make the greatest impact or do the most good?**

Once you uncover your strengths, keep in mind that you can manifest them in many ways, and numerous jobs will allow you to flex your most outstanding skills. Start by considering industries or functions that meet the criteria you defined in the exercise above, but don't get stuck in "all or nothing" thinking—especially in the job search. Various paths can lead to your dream job, and you may not even know what that is until you try it.

How to Find a Job

Networking

Believe it or not, "weak ties" are the best ties for finding a job, and according to an MIT study[55] of more than 20 million LinkedIn users, the reason is fairly straightforward. People you don't know well are typically outside your social circles and are, therefore, aware of opportunities that wouldn't otherwise come your way. So, don't only reach out to your close circles for job opportunities; be willing to cast a wider net.

Start the networking process by asking for informational meetings rather than job interviews. If you're interested in a specific employer or industry, ask to be connected to people working in those areas. Yes, people are busy, but most will be willing to spare 15 to 20 minutes to describe their job and career progression to you. (Hint: Most people love talking about themselves and their successes.) Always do your research beforehand. You don't need to stalk anyone on the internet; instead, check out their LinkedIn profile and be prepared with a few questions.

Guess what? These informational interviews aren't only for people who are starting their careers. They're also great for anyone who's changing careers or who's interested in advancing to the next level. Here are some examples of questions I keep in my back pocket for such interactions.

Questions for Informational Interviews

- Can you tell me more about how you got where you are today? Did you take courses in a related field or learn on the job?
- What skills or characteristics are essential to succeed in this role/function/industry?
- What do you love about your job?
- What resources can you recommend for someone interested in this job/company/industry? (For example, publications, volunteer work, events, etc.)
- Can you recommend anyone else I should speak with to learn more?

This last question is my favorite because it expands your network even more, and when you reach out to this new connection, you can say you have a referral. This approach beats cold calling any day, and most people are willing to meet with someone who's been recommended by a friend or acquaintance. (Hooray for weak ties!)

Applying for Jobs

Two schools of thought predominate when it comes to applying for jobs. One is the "laser-focus" approach, and the other is the "shotgun" method. The first involves identifying and homing in on your dream organization or role. The latter is more of a "numbers game," an approach Dan Miller presents in his book *48 Days to the Work You Love*.[56]

I've used both methods, and they can both yield results. However, your success will directly correlate with the time and effort you commit to your job search, whichever approach

NOTES

you choose. Below is the process I recommend, which is a combination of the two methods.

1. **Start with a list of companies or jobs you're interested in and apply to those first.** Then, reach out to anyone you know at those firms or in similar roles and ask for more information.

2. **Research companies and roles similar to those on your list and continue applying.**

3. Now that your prospective job opportunities have broadened, **set notifications across as many job-posting and career-building websites as possible.** Once you do that, you'll have a steady stream of leads in your inbox each day.

4. **Work with recruiters.** Research recruiting firms that specialize in your areas of interest and upload your resume to their websites. Recruiters can be an excellent resource for jobs that aren't yet publicly listed or that have an immediate hiring need.

5. **Set a daily and weekly quota for submitting job applications.** Meet or exceed those numbers and try to apply for jobs as soon as they're posted.

6. Don't stop there! **Continue your informational interviews,** especially at the companies you're actively pursuing.

7. **Look for small, lesser-known organizations in industries that interest you.** Go to their websites and search for open roles. Not all companies post jobs on major websites, and you'll have a better shot at a firm that doesn't receive an overwhelming number of applicants through one of the many job portals.

As a hiring manager, I know how overwhelming it can be to receive hundreds of job applications in my inbox over a very short time. If one of my colleagues knows and recommends someone whose resume is in that pile, chances are I'll give them an interview. Don't underestimate the importance of referrals in your job search, *especially* in large organizations that receive hundreds of thousands of applications annually.

Application Materials

Today's application materials go beyond a traditional resume, cover letter, and recommendations. They often include social media profiles, a personal website, and a work portfolio, depending on your industry. So, remember to present a consistent brand image everywhere. For example, be sure the information presented on your resume is consistent with your LinkedIn profile and so on.

Do everything you can to perfect your resume and cover letter and to make your public social profiles pristine. Triple-check your resume and cover letter for spelling and grammar errors, and reach out to experts for help. Your college or university likely has a career development center, so send them your application materials and ask for feedback. Most university career centers also assist alumni, so stay connected and ask for assistance even if it's been a while since you graduated. I found this resource extremely helpful when I was changing industries as a mid-career professional. For example, my counselor scanned my resume and analyzed it for keywords that would improve my chances of getting noticed for management and consulting roles in my field. She also helped me format my resume more effectively.

Employers will look at your social media profiles and online presence, so I recommend making all of your social profiles—except for LinkedIn—private, at least during your job search. Use LinkedIn as the online version of your resume

NOTES

and cover letter, and be active on the platform, as it's likely to lead you to potential opportunities and contacts.

Interviewing

Let's say your application was successful, and you've been invited for an interview. Now the real work begins. In my opinion, you can never be over-prepared for a job interview.

Below are the areas you need to research before the big day.

- **Study the company.** Scour the company website. Know when the company was founded and by whom. Know who the current leaders are. Be aware of existing customers, clients, initiatives, market trends, and news stories. Understand the target market. Who are the firm's competitors? What are the current pain points? What is the company doing well?
  Pro Tip: If you really want to learn about a company, check out the investor relations materials typically linked on the company website.

- **Know your intention.** Why do you admire this firm? Why do you want to work for them? What unique skills or perspectives can you bring to the job role?

- **Understand the role.** Study the job description. Think of ways you've demonstrated the attributes required. Prepare specific examples and stories that show you're qualified for the job. If any portion of the job description is unclear, ask for clarification during the interview.

- **Research your interviewer.** Ask for the name of your interviewer(s) before meeting with them and look them up on the company website and LinkedIn. Read any industry-related articles they've published and listen to recordings of panels or podcasts on which they've spoken. Look for common connections like hometowns, universities, professional organizations, and more.

"Tell Me About Yourself"

The chance of the interview opening this way is about 99.9%, so don't be at a loss for words. Have your elevator pitch polished and ready. Your answer should be a brief description of your background (education or experience), your current goal or objective, and anything else noteworthy or interesting about you. Limit this response to three to six sentences initially, leaving room for follow-up questions. Also, know that while you shouldn't adjust your resume for each job you apply for, you most certainly can tune your pitch. Use your research to customize your response.

Let me share my most recent answer to this question so you understand the gist of a good elevator pitch.

I'm a former Foreign Service Officer with a passion for public service and higher education. I have a master's degree in International Relations and an MBA specializing in International Business. As Executive Director of Strategic Initiatives, I built a team and launched a new business line that grosses more than $10M annually, taking my organization from cash flow negative to cash flow positive in less than a year.

Over the past five years, I've learned a lot about change management, and after a very successful change implementation, I'm eager for my next challenge.

This pitch covers a lot of ground in a few sentences. It encompasses my background, accomplishments, interests, and strengths—and it sparks a follow-up conversation. For example, my interviewer may be interested in knowing more about the Foreign Service, my current role, or why I'm looking to make a change. Either way, my pitch opens the doors to more questions about me and my experience (questions I know the answers to!) and increases the likelihood of a more organic conversation. Give your interviewers material they can work with, and the process will be more enjoyable for you both.

Below is my formula for the perfect interview elevator pitch.

"TELL ME ABOUT YOURSELF" FORMULA:

1. **Your Past:** One or two sentences about your education or experience.
2. **Your Present:** One or two sentences about your current skills or recent accomplishments. In other words, what you have to offer.
3. **Your Future:** One or two sentences about your interests, career goals, or current objective. (Try to frame this in the context of the job and company with which you're interviewing.)

Let's look at some other top interview questions. Be prepared to answer all of the following questions, and start by practicing your answers out loud, eliminating any filler words such as "like," "um," and "uh." Then, continue to repeat and refine your answers until they flow articulately, and you feel comfortable and confident with your responses. This process is very similar to how I'll teach you to prepare for exams in the next chapter: Recite your answers aloud from memory, then rinse and repeat until you recall every bullet point for each topic with ease.

Common Interview Questions

- **Tell me about yourself.** See the example above and remember the background-accomplishments-interests formula.
- **Why do you want to work for this company?** If it's a smaller company, they might ask, "How did you hear about us?"
- **What are your strengths?** You should know the answer to this question if you completed the exercise at the start of this chapter.
- **What are your areas of growth, development, or weakness, and how do you mitigate them?** Even if they don't ask how you mitigate weaknesses, I strongly encourage you to include this information in your answer.
- **What do you like least/most about your current job?** This is typically another way of asking the two previous questions.
- **Where do you see yourself in five years?** Hint: Pick a role within the firm. Avoid saying you want to be at a different company or working for yourself in five years.
- **Describe yourself in three words.** This question may be phrased, "How would you describe your personal brand?"
- **What makes you unique?** I hope you're starting to understand why knowing yourself is just as important as understanding the role.
- **Tell me about a time you exhibited (leadership/innovation/creativity/initiative/going the extra mile) in a past role?** Have specific examples of all of the above in mind in case you're asked.
- **Why are you leaving your current job?** Be careful with this one. Try not to say anything negative about

your current manager or employer. Also, be prepared with an explanation for any gaps in your resume. It's okay to take time off; just have something to show for it—even if it's volunteer work at an elephant sanctuary while traveling through Thailand. (I did that, by the way, and I highly recommend it.)

- **Do you have any questions for me?** We'll look at this question in greater detail below.

Chances are, you'll be asked at least a few of the above questions, which means you have no excuse for not being prepared for them. Last, but not least, don't forget to LISTEN during your interviews. Often, interviewers give clues about what they're looking for and what's important to the company. So, listen closely and tailor your responses accordingly. Now, I'll offer a few pointers on some of the questions above, and then it's your turn to practice, practice, practice!

Strengths and Weaknesses

If you're like most people, you can easily identify your strengths, but it's not as fun to share your weaknesses. I loathed this question for years until someone finally explained it to me. Probably noticing the grimace on my face, a senior-level manager shared the following during a job interview. "We don't ask this question because we're looking for the perfect employee. We know no one is perfect, and everyone has their strengths and weaknesses. We ask about weaknesses because first, we want to know that you're self-aware. Second, we want to know how you mitigate your weaknesses."

I couldn't have said it better myself, and when I think about the question in those terms, it doesn't bother me as much. Just like everyone else, I have my pros and cons. Yet, I work hard to position myself in my areas of strength, and for arenas where

I'm not the best, I partner with people who are. That strategy shows self-awareness. I don't let my weaknesses get the better of me, and most of all, I don't let my organization's mission suffer. Instead, I find ways to leverage my team's strengths so, together, we produce our best work.

I'm sure you also have ways to overcome your natural weak points and allow your strengths to shine. Focus on those positive attributes and mitigation strategies when you answer this question.

Questions for the Interviewer

You can count on the interviewer closing the meeting by asking if you have any questions. Avoid saying you don't have questions; otherwise, it may appear you're not interested in the company. (If the interview has been more of a discussion format and you've been asking questions all along, that's different.) However, you should also be mindful of your interviewer's time; don't extend the interview length with a litany of questions.

Rather, be prepared with a short list of questions about the company for which the answers aren't available on the website. Good topics to consider are company culture, organizational leadership, shifting dynamics, upcoming challenges, and opportunities for training and development. Additional questions may arise during the interview—be sure to jot those down so you don't forget them at the end. Finally, confirm that you thoroughly understand the role. For example, you might want to ask who you would report to, who else you'd work with, and what the onboarding process is like. Pick two or three of your most burning questions; you can always follow up with additional questions after the interview or once you've received a job offer.

Avoid asking about salary or benefits. The Human Resources representative will review this information with you when you get the offer. If you can't think of anything else to ask, a great question to end with is, "What are the next steps in the process?" This query demonstrates that you're still interested in the role and engaged in the recruitment process.

After the Interview

It's polite to thank your interviewers for their time, so don't neglect this step or wait too long to express gratitude. Instead, send your thank-you message within 24 to 48 hours. Doing so is a great way to stay on the interview panel's radar and is a chance to ask any questions you may have forgotten during the interview. A follow-up email is also an excellent opportunity to provide more information or clarification on a specific question posed during the interview, especially if you didn't represent yourself the way you wanted to with one of your answers.

Since you asked about next steps during your interview, you should have a sense of when you'll hear back. If you don't hear back within the appointed time frame, it's perfectly acceptable to follow up by phone or email. Keep your communication friendly and brief—simply let your contact know you're still interested in the role.

How to Keep a Job

Congratulations! All your hard work and preparation paid off, and you got the job! Now, all you have to do is keep it. The following tips will help you manage the workplace well. Remember the rules for professionalism we learned in Chapter 6? Embody those rules in every professional interaction. As a reminder, here they are again, adapted for the workplace.

✓ Dress professionally.

✓ Be punctual.

✓ Demonstrate confidence.

✓ Be prepared.

✓ Be engaged.

✓ Be present.

✓ Act with Integrity.

✓ Own your mistakes and learn from them.

THE RULES OF PROFESSIONALISM	
DRESS PROFESSIONALLY	Always be clean, neat, and well-groomed. Every industry and organization has a unique dress code, so look to your organization's leaders for cues on how to best present yourself. Always dress for the job you want, not the one you have!
BE PUNCTUAL	Better yet, be early! Whether online or in person, make it a habit to arrive for meetings and events a few minutes early. Punctuality demonstrates respect for others and their time. As a bonus, those extra minutes before a meeting provide an excellent opportunity to get to know your colleagues. With the shift to remote work, the Zoom room is the new water cooler, so make the most of any opportunity for small talk and interpersonal connection.

DEMONSTRATE CONFIDENCE	Nonverbal communication, such as eye contact, good posture, voice projection, clear enunciation, and a firm handshake, speak volumes. These cues signal confidence, even if you don't always feel that way inside. Good posture, for example, conveys confidence and attentiveness and is also good for your health. Conversely, reclining in the office communicates slothfulness and a lack of engagement, and slouching at your desk can strain and fatigue your muscles unnecessarily. You'll look and feel better if you sit and stand up straight (even if you're on a video call).
BE PREPARED	Be prepared for every meeting you attend. Do your homework in advance. Anticipate any questions you might receive and come prepared with answers. If you're leading the meeting, have an agenda and share it with attendees in advance. Then, assign a notetaker and share the minutes from the meeting afterward. Always meet deadlines. If you encounter a roadblock, raise the concern *before* it becomes a more significant issue.

BE ENGAGED	When you're in meetings or collaborating with colleagues, close your laptop and take notes on a notepad so you're not tempted to answer emails or surf the web. Lean forward and listen when others speak. Support colleagues' ideas using verbal and nonverbal feedback. Speak up when you have information that can benefit the group. If meeting minutes are required, offer to be the official notetaker. Never leave a meeting without summarizing action items or asking for the next steps.
BE PRESENT	When you're at work, be fully focused on work. Put your phone away. Give your colleagues, clients, and customers your complete attention. Look them in the eye. Become an active listener by paraphrasing requests, instructions, and concerns. If you're struggling to focus, first remove all distractions. If that doesn't work, try a device-free walk or a two-minute meditation to help reset your attention.

NOTES

ACT WITH INTEGRITY	Always do the right thing. I define integrity as doing the right thing when nobody's watching. No matter your occupation, industry, or career level, you will be faced with opportunities to act unethically or perhaps illegally. As your career progresses, ethical issues become more complex and their ramifications more severe. The more you practice honesty and integrity with every decision you make, the more automatic it becomes, which is why making good decisions at every level of your career is so important.
LEARN FROM MISTAKES	You're not perfect. No one is. You will make mistakes, and when you do, the best way to handle them is to acknowledge and take ownership of the issue. Then craft a solution so the problem never happens again. Don't wait for your manager to come to you when you make a mistake. If you know you've screwed up, reach out first and ask how you can do better next time. Or, let your boss know that you've remedied the situation and it won't happen again.

How to Advance Your Career

Tooting Your Own Horn

Most of us don't like to admit it, but to advance in our careers, we need to "toot our own horn" occasionally. Doing so can be difficult for many reasons. For instance, some of us (particularly women, according to Helgesen and Goldsmith)[57], worry we'll sound conceited or not be considered team players if we tout our own accomplishments. But here's the rub: You can't receive credit for your wins if no one knows about them. (I remind my direct reports of this fact frequently.) So, allow me to share some practical ways to communicate your success without becoming an insufferable braggart. *And for those of you who don't have a problem tooting your horn, your challenge is to infuse humility into your conversations, share recognition with others, and appropriately attribute sources of good ideas and work.*

The best way to share your excellent work is in your weekly one-on-one with your manager (more on this topic below). Another tangible way to showcase your achievements is with a weekly roundup. I usually share workplace highlights with leaders and supervisors at the end of the week, so they know what my teams and I have contributed during that time.

In addition to a weekly report, I also like to keep a separate list of successes for the year (I call this my "highlights reel"). This list includes long-term projects or initiatives, significant accomplishments, new business acquired, or challenges overcome. I typically share this list with my career coach or supervisor before my annual review. I maintain and update the list throughout the year, so I don't forget any substantial contributions at year's end.

Another way to boost your professional profile is to take advantage of any speaking or presenting opportunities that come your way. Whether your audience is internal or external, presenting is an excellent way to showcase your expertise or perspective and build your credibility within an organization. Never turn down an opportunity to speak to an audience (even if it's at the last minute), provided you have time to prepare. Always draft talking points in advance. Use your newfound outlining skills to sketch out your remarks; then practice your

NOTES

opening and closing statements so you begin and end with confidence.

Lastly, remember, it's okay to use the word "I" if you accomplished a particularly impressive initiative on your own. I learned this truth from a former supervisor and mentor, Jim Gash, who also wrote the foreword for this book. He offered the following advice: "Don't say 'we,' say 'I.' You did this incredible work, and it's okay to take credit for it." *Amen to that!*

The Magic of the One-on-One

According to McKinsey, bosses play a huge role in employee happiness. In fact, relationships with management are the top factor in employee job satisfaction.[58]

If you're under the same impression I used to be—that the best boss is the one you never see—think again. In my opinion, one of the best things you can do for your career and your relationship with your supervisor is to meet regularly. This "one-on-one" should occur every week. It's a time to create a work plan for the upcoming week, report any issues, and ask questions. If your manager doesn't have time for a weekly one-on-one, think about creative ways to keep the lines of communication open. Your strategy can include a weekly email, as discussed earlier, or more spontaneous check-ins. Remember, the one-on-one is the perfect opportunity to share your achievements, ask for advice, and seek feedback, which leads me to my next point.

Seeking Feedback

Feedback has a bad rap. While we all probably cringe a little at the thought of constructive criticism, I think the real problem is that we don't receive feedback often enough to normalize it. The less feedback we receive, the scarier it is, and the more we try to avoid it. But what if we actively sought others' input instead? In fact, it's best to seek feedback from multiple, diverse perspectives.

One of the best things I learned in my MBA program was how to receive feedback, and guess what? Whether the feedback is positive or negative, accurate or inaccurate, and no matter what your critic's intentions are, the proper way to receive feedback is to look your critic in the eye and say sincerely, "Thank you for your feedback."

That's it. Don't argue or offer a rebuttal. Over time, you'll probably find that even (and especially) the people you disagree with the most have valuable information you can use to improve. So, ask for feedback early and often and practice a gracious response until it becomes automatic. A simple way to do this is by asking some version of the following question at the end of every one-on-one: "Is there anything else I can do to be helpful to you, this organization, or our mission?"

Managing Up

It doesn't matter what your role in the company is or where your position falls on the organizational chart—it's your job to raise red flags (and potential opportunities) to your supervisors. For example, if your team is at risk of missing a deadline, let your manager know *beforehand*. If you observe an upset or angry client or customer, don't keep that information to yourself. If you see a workplace trainwreck about to occur, escalate the situation to management immediately. While your supervisors may not be able to stop the collision entirely, you'd better believe they'll appreciate a heads-up allowing them to mitigate damage and take charge of the narrative. While you may not be in a position to remove a roadblock, your managers usually are (in fact, that's their job), so never sit on information that can benefit the team or the organization. Instead, raise appropriate concerns or opportunities sooner rather than later, and if possible, be prepared with thoughtful options, so you can be part of a dynamic solution.

Make Friends and Allies

While a bad boss may be a primary reason people leave a job,[59] having a best friend at work is a big reason employees stay. According to Gallup data, in addition to boosting retention, having a best friend at work also increases engagement, company profitability, and job success.[60] So, if you want to make your workplace more enjoyable and be more successful, start making friends—and don't stop there. In addition to a best bud, look for and actively cultivate allies.

Allies are colleagues in a position to help you—and vice versa. They often share your perspective on the company's future needs or direction. They may have a similar role as yours but in a different business unit. To develop these relationships, share information and resources freely. Loop in colleagues who aren't directly related to a project, communication, or event but who will benefit from awareness of it. Develop productive cross-departmental relationships as well as good rapport with vendors and clients.

Lastly, nurture relationships above, below, and across the organizational chart. Rather than thinking about what you can gain from an association, ask how you can be of service to others.

Mentorship

Something the most successful people in the world have in common, according to psychologist Mihaly Csikszentmihalyi, is a mentor.[61] Mentors do more than offer career advice; they can also provide emotional support and much-needed perspective, particularly if they work outside your organization. Mentors typically have more experience in a given field than you do. Mentors are role models.

The wonderful thing about mentorship is that it can and should happen organically. Sure, your employer might have a mentorship or coaching program, but the best mentor-mentee relationships form informally over time. I recommend looking for someone who has your best interests at heart *and* who will tell you the unadulterated truth (rather than what you want to hear) so you have the opportunity to grow and improve. You should continue using the networking skills you learned at the beginning of this chapter, not just to find jobs, but to find mentors throughout your career.

Once you have a mentor, the best way to "pay it forward" is to mentor others. No matter how much or how little experience you have, someone can always learn from you, so share your knowledge and insights with others and watch your sphere of influence expand. You might be surprised to find that you can learn from your mentees' perspectives as well, which will help you be a more insightful and inclusive leader.

My Story

Many people have asked me how I accomplished the most challenging goals in my life, such as becoming a diplomat at the age of twenty-four, working for a Big Four consulting firm, and writing a book. The answer is simple, but not easy. I used the steps in this book to achieve my dreams, AND I didn't give up.

First, I identified my goal and shared it with others. Then, I learned what I needed to do to accomplish it. From there, I made a plan (for example, preparing for the Foreign Service Exam or the case study portion of a consulting interview). Then, I removed all distractions and used the skills I taught you in this book to master the knowledge required.

While that might sound easy, I dedicated eight to 12 hours a day, for weeks, months, and sometimes years on end, to make my dreams come true. I put in the time and effort and poured my soul into these endeavors. Much like a professional athlete, I over-prepared so that when it was time to perform, I was on autopilot.

None of my dreams came true overnight. In fact, they started as dreams but transformed into goals as I operationalized them with careful planning. Most of the time, as I learned more about my career objectives, I discovered I needed additional knowledge or new skills, so I invested the time and money to develop those talents. Sometimes, exploring career options through classes, workshops, or even jobs made me realize certain professional paths were not for me.

What's more, saying "yes" to my dream often meant saying "no" to other things. For example, when I was a design student, while most of my friends were on exotic vacations during spring break, I was at the Santa Monica Library, studying the legal requirements to start a business in California. While it wasn't as fun as a trip to Aruba, I wouldn't change this decision. When you have a clear vision of what you want to accomplish, you'll understand that tradeoffs are an essential part of achieving your goals, and you won't regret the sacrifices you make to get to the next step.

> ***You cannot expect success without sacrifice, and you cannot be afraid to fail.***

You cannot expect success without sacrifice, and you cannot be afraid to fail. Without exception, my life's greatest accomplishments involved multiple attempts, or what some might call "failure." But I prefer to think of these false starts as iterations, not the end of the journey, but part of the process—

and you should too. For instance, I took the Foreign Service Exam three times before I was finally offered a position as a U.S. diplomat. In addition, I've spent more than a decade writing and refining a novel I still haven't published, but working on that book instilled in me the skills and discipline to write this one, and I'm confident one day I'll share my novel with you too.

Despite setbacks, both personally and professionally, I never gave up. Failure is a wonderful teacher, especially if you use it as fuel to supercharge a more focused and knowledgeable leg of your journey. I share this with you because I want you to achieve your dreams too, and if you follow the advice in this book, you'll have a roadmap for doing difficult things well.

The Trail Versus the Ladder

Career progression is more like a winding trail than a ladder. It will have summits and valleys, but every step along the path will teach you something you need for the journey. Sometimes your destination may seem out of sight, and that's okay, as long as you continue putting one foot in front of the other. In fact, the best advice I have ever received is to simply "walk it forward," so I offer you the same guidance for your career.

Career progression is more like a winding trail than a ladder.

First, decide what you want to do, then share your goal with others. Doing so not only creates accountability but it also helps you find like-minded companions for the journey. Then, walk it forward—step by step and day by day. You won't know if a career path is right for you until you try it, so take baby steps toward your goal each day, and remember, small daily gains will outpace inconsistent growth every time.

NOTES

CAREER PLANNING ACTIVITY: DREAM BIG

Writing about and sharing your goals has power, so in this exercise, I want you to dream big! First, write down up to three professional goals (or potential career paths) below, then share them with your friends and family.

While it might seem scary to commit to an intention by putting it in writing and sharing it with others, both actions increase the likelihood of you achieving your dream because they create accountability. You can even share your career goals with me on social media using the hashtag: #getthedegree.

Extra Credit: Your goals will be even more effective if you make them SMART (Specific, Measurable, Achievable, Relevant, Time-bound). See the Appendix for more on SMART goals.

My Professional Goals

1.

2.

3.

CHAPTER 14

The Last Lesson

"Everybody dies, but not everybody lives."

~ DRAKE

If you've implemented the suggestions in this book, you should be planning your time, using it efficiently, and creating habits that make studying (almost) automatic. Up to this point, we've focused largely on what to do. Now, I want you to shift your focus inward, on how to *be*. The following tips for achieving balance will provide perspective and help you stay engaged with your goals from beginning to end. Most academic programs are more like marathons than sprints; they require a consistent, dedicated effort to succeed. If you follow this chapter's advice, you'll be less likely to burn out and more likely to cross the finish line with a flourish.

Be Curious

You, and only you, are responsible for your education. How much time and thoughtful energy you dedicate to your studies directly correlates with the amount of knowledge and mastery

You, and only you, are responsible for your education.

you'll gain. Furthermore, to make the most of your formal education, your intellectual curiosity should extend beyond the classroom and into the "real" world of practice and application. Following are the tips I use to help me round out my textbook knowledge with practical insights.

Podcasts, YouTube, and Audiobooks

To help me widen my learning scope, I'll typically look for podcasts, newsletters, YouTube videos, and audiobooks related to the subjects I'm currently studying. For example, if I'm studying finance and economics, I'll subscribe to a weekly podcast or newsletter on those topics. (Hint: Look for content from primary sources such as news and government agencies, NGOs, and think tanks.) Then, I'll try to connect what I learn through these sources to what I'm learning in the classroom. Not only does this process introduce me to real-time examples of theoretical principles, but the current events covered often also provide rich fodder for research papers and class discussions.

On the flip side, if I'm struggling to understand a concept, I'll search for YouTube videos that break it down. A number of lectures by leading professors are available online for free, but I often find fellow students sharing their knowledge online even more helpful. Finally, audiobooks are another excellent way to supplement your understanding. I almost always listen to an audiobook that complements whatever topic I'm learning or researching at the moment. This practice illuminates my studies and enhances my academic and professional work.

Talk to Practitioners

I can't overstate the importance of talking to practitioners in the field you're studying. If you're taking an accounting course, chat with your accountant about the realities of her job. If you're studying business law, take your lawyer friends to lunch and learn about contracts. If you're struggling with your Information Systems class, reach out to your IT buddy and ask him to explain what "the cloud" really is. (Yes, I actually did this.)

Textbook theories can only take you so far. When you delve beneath their surface, you'll find most subject areas are far more complex in practice than we've been taught and are often littered with contradictions academic texts might gloss over in an effort to present a flawless conceptual model. These contradictions aren't bad; they can offer you a deeper understanding of the subject and resolve gaps in your learning. Conversely, you may also find areas of practice that perfectly mirror your classroom knowledge. Dig into these spaces to gain an even deeper understanding. In my experience, many academic journals assume expert-level knowledge of a topic. So, if you're a student learning a new concept for the first time, you may find yourself a little lost, which is when speaking to a practitioner can help illuminate ideas and connect the dots through lessons only learned on the job.

When you're seeking additional knowledge or input, look for reliable sources to shed light on and clarify what you already know. Remember, your education is in your hands, so make the most of it any way you can.

Be Present

You've undoubtedly heard this phrase before. It might even be hanging on your wall or printed on your coffee mug, but the notion of being present is far more than a cliché. Mindfulness has the power to transform your work, your relationships, and your life if you practice it vigilantly. The meditation, breathwork, and gratitude practices suggested in this book can help.

According to research, the ability to be "mindfully present" ranks highest among 33 leadership traits.[62] Additionally, a Harvard survey of more than 1,000 leaders found that a mindful presence is a crucial strategy for engaging others, fostering better relationships, and improving performance.[63] While I know it's tempting to multitask when you have a lot on your plate, I encourage you to develop the habit of being fully present no matter where you are.

When you're at work, be fully focused on work. When you're in class, don't let anything distract you from the lecture. When you're at home, give your family or housemates the attention they deserve. We now know that multitasking is a myth; people are more effective when they focus intently on one activity at a time. So, understand that mindful presence facilitates focus, and focus is your superpower—it enables you to do more (work) with less (time). Being present also helps you enjoy and reap the benefits of another critical factor to success: rest.

Be Refreshed

Rest and recovery are essential. Not only does sleep help solidify learning and improve cognitive performance,[64] but according to research, rest also restores focus.[65] Just like a muscle, the brain can become fatigued from focused attention, and the best way to relieve that tension is to rest. Please note, however, that rest comes in many forms, and physical rest, including sleep, is just one of them. In fact, according to Dr. Dalton-Smith, author of *Sacred Rest*, the seven types of rest are: physical, mental, spiritual, emotional, sensory, social, and creative.[66] Additionally, it shouldn't come as a surprise that the best place to rejuvenate is in nature. "Ecotherapy" can reduce cognitive load, decrease stress and anxiety, and help us regain focus and composure.

My formula for mental restoration is first to work hard and give it your all, and then rest in the following intervals.

- **Daily:** Give yourself a short "brain break" after one to two hours of focused study. During that time, don't look at any digital device screens. If you can, go for a quick walk.
- **Nightly:** Aim for seven to eight hours of sleep each night.[67]
- **Weekly:** Take one day off each week to rest. Don't engage in any formal work or study on that day.
- **Quarterly:** Go away for a weekend once per academic term. Do your homework in advance, so you can enjoy a getaway or a study-free staycation.
- **Annually:** Take at least one or two weeks per year for vacation (more if you can). Visit friends and family. See someplace new.

The most important thing to remember during these rest intervals is to unplug and do things that refresh and rejuvenate you. This will be different for everyone. Recreation can include musical, artistic, or creative endeavors, travel, reading, volunteer work, and even exhilarating experiences like mountain climbing, skydiving, skiing, or scuba.

> ### *Recreation resets the mind and energizes the body.*

Recreation resets the mind and energizes the body. So, don't neglect time with family and friends (even though you'll be tempted to do so), and don't neglect your physical and spiritual practices. Caring for your mind, body, and spirit is restorative. You're on this journey for the long haul, so if you want to go the distance, you must pace yourself accordingly. This means taking appropriate breaks and getting the restoration you need to stay healthy, happy, and motivated.

NOTES

Put quality time and effort into your studies, so you can rest and rejuvenate fully, knowing that the time you take to refresh yourself will only benefit your work. Consider the words of Dr. Phillip L. Pointer, "Rest is not an occasional reward for good work. Rest is a prerequisite for good work."

Be Still

When life gets tough, go inward.

> ### *When life gets tough, go inward.*

As much as I wish this weren't true, a time will probably come when you'll feel so stressed (be it from work, school, personal life, or all three) you can't think straight. When you're in this state of acute overwhelm, the prefrontal cortex shuts down, resulting in a sense of panic or paralysis.[68] As a fully-employed MBA student with a lot of responsibility on my shoulders, I knew this feeling well; however, I also knew that if I wanted to be effective, I needed to overcome it.

Now, when I start to enter that state of overwhelm where my brain feels too flooded by tasks or emotions to do anything, I turn to meditation. Meditation has been a lifesaver for me in my personal, professional, and academic life. This regular practice keeps me grounded and helps me stay focused when I need it most.

Not only does meditation reduce stress and anxiety, but over time, a regular mindfulness practice can also improve attention and concentration.[69] All of these benefits are essential to your success as a student. If you don't meditate already, consider starting with a guided practice available on an app such as Calm or Headspace. As you continue your practice, you may wish to move from guided to non-guided meditation, and the length of time you meditate may increase. However, in a "meltdown moment," I find that even two to five minutes of breathwork is enough to calm my nerves and help me refocus. (You'll learn a helpful breathing technique in the section below.) Once you experience meditation's benefits, you may choose to make it more than an emergency coping measure and instead incorporate a daily practice into your life, as I do now.

Be Purposeful

Sometimes a lack of clarity can also cause anxiety. Whenever I feel that I lack direction, I often go back to my strengths to remind myself of my purpose and reset my focus. Knowing your strengths is essential for you as a student because it helps you focus your time and energy on areas where you can be the most effective and successful.

Some of my favorite inventories are the Myers-Briggs Type Indicator (MBTI) and the "CliftonStrengths" assessment illuminated in the bestselling book *StrengthsFinder 2.0*. Many college and university career centers offer similar assessments. I strongly encourage you to take one, and then continue taking them and referencing them throughout your life. Your skills and interests will likely transform, as will the job market.

> *Purpose is powerful.*

Purpose is powerful, and knowing—and believing—you are gifted with unique talents and are here to do something special fuels the internal drive and motivation you need to be successful. While finding your purpose in life is a subject for an entirely separate book, what I can tell you here is that knowing your strengths is the first step in that process. I often return to my strengths when I'm feeling lost or discouraged. Not only does revisiting and recognizing my innate abilities encourage me, but it also reminds me that I'm here for a purpose. For instance, I know my strengths are learning, teaching, and writing, so I use my voice (the written word) to communicate knowledge and wisdom to others. This knowledge is what compelled me to write this book and gave me the motivation to complete it, even when I faced obstacles. If you need help finding this same sense of purpose and direction, go back and review the "Finding Career Direction" exercise at the beginning of the last chapter.

If you're struggling or feeling lost, studying your strengths may reveal that you're not utilizing your best assets. If that's the case, take the opportunity to reassess and redirect your efforts into work, studies, or volunteer activities within your areas of strength. Other times, assessing your gifts can inspire you to lean into them even more: to raise your hand and speak up; to volunteer to help others; to pick up an artistic elective or creative hobby; or to simply be bolder in offering the world the best you have to give.

Be Grateful

No matter where you are in your learning journey, you didn't get there alone. You likely have family or friends who have supported you (financially, emotionally, or otherwise). Perhaps a teacher or administrator encouraged you, offered personal or professional guidance, or wrote a letter of recommendation that helped you get where you are today. Whatever the case, don't wait until you graduate to say thank you.

No matter where you are in your learning journey, you didn't get there alone.

When I think about gratitude, the Bible story of the ten lepers often comes to mind. According to Scripture,[70] after Jesus healed all ten lepers, only one returned to express gratitude. What I love about this story is that it's so human. We all forget to be grateful at times, but I am reassured knowing that it is never too late (or too early, for that matter) to say thanks.

Action Item: If someone in your life has helped you get where you are today, take a moment right now to call, text, email, or send a thank-you card. Be specific when you describe how this benefactor has helped you and what the result or outcome was; they may not know the impact of their encouraging words or acts of kindness unless you share it.

Gratitude Exercise

☐ Think of someone who's helped you get where you are.
☐ Say "thank you" to that person TODAY.

Why am I talking about gratitude in a study skills book? Because we can't always change our circumstances, but the one thing we can control is our attitude. And sometimes, changing your attitude can change everything. Too often, especially when we feel overwhelmed, we focus on what we *don't* have (enough time, resources, brain power, etc.). Gratitude forces us to focus on what we *have*.

What's more, gratitude affects the part of the brain that controls higher-order thinking and focused attention, which means positivity can help you think critically and analytically. Don't believe me? Recall a time when you were overwhelmed by negative emotions. How hard was it to reason? According to Harvard-trained psychologist Daniel Goleman, positivity can result in more creative thinking, increased mental productivity, and a greater attention span.[71] (Did you catch that? Gratitude can help you study better and longer.) Additionally, gratitude and positivity spur the brain's production of serotonin and dopamine, which makes us feel happier and calmer, and activates the feel-good reward center in our brain. Also, because mindfulness decreases cortisol levels,[72] gratitude can help clear brain fog, increase focus, and reduce stress. So why not incorporate a daily gratitude practice into your life?

Be Calm

Do you know what else can reduce stress and cortisol (the primary stress hormone)? We've discussed some of the suggestions below already, but the entire list bears repeating because it's a reminder that your ultimate success as a student depends on how you nurture your mind, body, and spirit.

Ways to Lower Stress[73]

1. Sufficient Sleep
2. Regular Exercise
3. A Healthy Diet
4. Laughter, Fun, and Recreation
5. Time Spent in Nature
6. Healthy Relationships
7. Caring for Pets
8. Spirituality/Prayer
9. Deep Breathing
10. Mindfulness

Be Mindful

"Whether you think you can, or you think you can't—you're right." I couldn't agree more with Henry Ford on this matter of the mind.

One of the most incredible things about the brain is that it believes what you tell it. That's why the stories, mantras, affirmations, words, and thoughts we dwell on are crucial to the quality of our lives and our potential for success.

> **"Whether you think you can, or you think you can't—you're right." ~ Henry Ford**

I learned this principle early in life by performing in piano recitals beginning at age six. I remember recitals when every pianist performed impeccably. Then, of course, there were the painful ones. One student would "choke" early in the evening, and every subsequent performance would be riddled with missed notes, dissonant melodies, and the dreaded mid-sonata meltdown. As an advanced pianist among my peers, my piece was most often positioned as the show's finale, giving me ample time to stress out about my forthcoming performance and absorb and internalize the tendencies of the group that preceded me.

In those moments, as the butterflies in my stomach morphed from fluttering insects into bats beating their wings relentlessly against my abdomen, my mother would lean over and whisper to me about the "power of suggestion." My Latina "tiger mom" would remind me that just because other students made mistakes didn't mean I had to. I had practiced, and I was prepared to succeed. My mother encouraged me not to let my mind or my nerves get the better of me, and guess what? Her promptings worked. A few timely words had the power to impact my performance for the best.

In fact, what my mother taught me about mastering my mind as a child not only serves me to this day, but it's also a principle employed by world-class athletes and high achievers across the globe. While we all experience anxiety under pressure, the best performers know how to *channel* nervous energy in a way that fuels performance rather than hinders it.

A great way to direct energy is through your breath. Hopefully, you're working on deep breathing techniques during your meditation practice, but if not, here are some tips. According to experts, it's the exhalation (and offloading of carbon dioxide), rather than the inhalation, that calms us the most. "Exhale-emphasized breathing," says Dr. Huberman, "leads to much more rapid activation of the calming arm of

NOTES

the nervous system."[74] So, the next time you need to get your nerves under control quickly, try the following breath cycle one to three times. You'll be amazed by the difference it makes.

Quick-Calming Breathing Technique

1. Sit up straight and exhale.
2. Take a deep double inhale through the nose (to the count of four).
3. Hold your breath and pause.
4. Now exhale fully through the mouth (to the count of eight).
5. Repeat the above two or three times.

Studies show that this diaphragmatic "deep sigh" is enough to reset the autonomic nervous system and switch your body from a hyperactive sympathetic (fight-or-flight) state to a more balanced parasympathetic (rest-and-digest) state.[75]

Be Prepared

I know from both personal experience and working with students that test anxiety is real. The good news is you can borrow a hack elite performers use to channel that nervous (potential) energy into useful (kinetic) energy by being prepared and shifting your mindset.

The best way to battle anxiety and self-doubt is to show up prepared. Knowing you've done everything you can to bring your best self to game day is crucial—studying hard, getting enough sleep, and practicing can all help. Additionally, recreating the conditions of an examination or important performance (such as a job interview) will also help tremendously. I call this a "stress rehearsal."

The Stress Rehearsal

Remember when I was a piano student learning to master stage fright? To prepare myself for the big day, I would spend a week practicing on the massive concert grand piano I would play during my performance. I realized that the touch of the keys and pedals differed from my small console piano at home, and I wanted to control for every possible variable in a stressful situation. Even though I knew I couldn't completely eliminate my nerves, I could get a feel for the instrument and the size of the room. I'd practice walking gracefully from my seat to the piano and back again (because who wants to trip and fall in front of an audience of their peers?). So when the big day finally came, and I sat down at the shiny, black, 10-foot piano with the heavy ivory keys, the experience wasn't new to me. I'd done it scores of times before, and now my only job was to repeat the process once again.

Interestingly, this exercise I practiced as a child is similar to the crisis management training some of the world's largest and most prominent organizations employ. For example, before sending me abroad as a Foreign Service Officer, the State Department required me and all new officers to role-play crisis situations. The U.S. Government invested the time and money to recreate realistic scenarios (including a mock prison cell) so that when we were in the field, and a real crisis erupted, we would know what to do. While the nerves in a situation like that might still be present, they wouldn't be debilitating because we had done this before. We practiced, we knew what to do, and we were prepared to perform in a high-stakes situation.

The same is true for test-taking. If you suffer from test anxiety, study like crazy, then do your best to recreate the exam conditions. Take a practice exam seated at a desk with no distractions and a timer counting down your minutes. Does that sound stressful? Well, examinations usually are, but the more you practice, the better you'll perform in a pinch. For example, if you know you'll have to write an essay during your final exam, time yourself whenever you complete a homework assignment and aim to improve your timing with each one. Or, give yourself practice essays so you can master the ability to organize your thoughts in a short amount of time.

According to Dr. Huberman,[76] you can overcome stress in one of two ways. One is to calm yourself down (through breathing, meditation, etc.), and the other is to build up your stress tolerance, which is why rehearsing high-pressure situations, or the "stress rehearsal," can prove helpful.

Exam Preparation

One of my favorite study hacks for examinations is trying to predict the test questions. I start by putting my "professor" cap on and imagining the questions I would ask if I were the instructor. First, I typically generate a list of terms or concepts I'll likely need to define or describe. Then, I select topics I suspect might be the subject of short-answer or essay questions. Once I have my list, I outline key themes within those subject areas and then talk myself through a cohesive response. (I speak the answers to my questions aloud to help reinforce the material.) These "talking points" will become the basis for an essay question response. If I can't sufficiently explain an idea out loud, I go back and review that concept before moving on. Finally, I review and rehearse the lists of bullet points under each topic until I can recall each subject area without looking at my notes.

Pro Tip: This "retrieval" study method is the key to successful test-taking. Challenging yourself to recall information from memory requires far more effort than passively skimming or reviewing notes, but this active form of study mirrors the conditions of most exams. For this reason, flashcards are the most simple, inexpensive, yet effective study tool. (Between us, I still use them today to help me quickly learn complex concepts and commit them to memory.)

FINAL EXAM "CHEAT" SHEET

1. **Read through your notes or textbook outline and highlight key terms and topics.** (See Chapter 5 for a refresher.)
2. **Make a list of all terms and concepts likely to be on the test.** Organize them in the order you learned them (by chapter or chronologically is usually best).
   a. **Key Definitions.** Rather than memorize a definition verbatim, identify two or three keywords that will help you remember and communicate the idea in your own words.
   b. **Key Concepts.** Make a bulleted list of three to five main points within a subject area.
3. **Practice your "answers."** Restate your key terms and concepts as questions, then talk yourself through a hypothetical response as you review your notes.
4. **Identify learning gaps.** If you struggled to explain an idea, go back and reread the topic in the original text. Add clarifying information to your bulleted study guide, then rehearse your hypothetical "answer" until it flows easily.
5. **Test yourself.** Now, practice your responses *without looking at your notes.* Can you recall every bullet point for each major topic—and expound upon each point—without any assistance? If so, you're well prepared for your exam.

Speaking of exams, now is the perfect time to reflect on everything you've just learned.

The Final Exam

At this point, most authors would offer a summary of the book's key themes, but what I think are the most important concepts doesn't matter. What *you've* learned and can apply to your life starting today is what matters most. So, let's call this assignment your "final exam." (Did you really think I'd let you go without one last quiz?) I want you to put the active reading skills you learned in Chapter 5 to work and write three to five tips you've learned from this book that you will implement in your life, work, or studies.

FINAL EXERCISE:
Write three to five key takeaways or learnings from this book below.
1.
2.
3.
4.
5.
List three to five tips, tricks, tools, or "hacks" you will implement into your life or studies. *Hint: These should be action items.*
1.
2.
3.
4.
5.

Great job! But you're not done yet. Whenever you feel overwhelmed, I want you to do the following things.

The Overwhelm Antidote

1. Take a deep breath and an even bigger sigh. Do that once more.
2. Go back to your "why" from Exercise 1 and visualize completing your ultimate goal.
3. Revisit the key takeaways you've just written and ask yourself which ones are missing from your current approach.
4. Based on your answer, define your "next step." (Refer to Chapter 11 for a refresher on the Next Step Methodology.)

I guarantee this exercise will help you find the motivation, clarity, and, most importantly, the next step to managing your workload.

Now, just in case you were wondering, here is my response to the final exam questions.

My Key Takeaways

- Keep an eye on your "why."
- "Measure twice, cut once." Plan and prioritize.
- Remember how to eat an elephant. (One bite at a time!)
- Work hard, then rest and rejuvenate.
- Reward yourself for a job well done.

Tools I Will Use

- I will incorporate a daily gratitude practice.
- I will commit to a five-minute meditation each morning.
- I will practice deep breathing techniques daily.
- I will actively seek mentors and mentor others.

- I will share this book and its insights with anyone who needs it.

Be Fearless

Don't be afraid of what you don't know—embrace it! The space between what you know and what you don't is precisely where learning occurs. You've invested time, money, and considerable energy into your education, so don't squander it. If you don't understand something, ask for help. Don't plagiarize or try to fake what you don't know; you'll only be cheating yourself. To demonstrate this principle, I'll end with one last story.

During the penultimate semester of my MBA program, I struggled to understand some of the concepts in one of my final courses, Global Macroeconomics. My midterm presentation for the course involved reading an academic article on macroeconomics and then relating it to lessons learned in class. I selected a well-written but highly complex piece from one of the field's leading experts. While I appreciated the thoroughness and organization of the piece, it was obviously written for fellow economists, not a layperson. I admit that parts of the article were completely over my head. I thought about choosing a less challenging piece because I knew if I stuck with my current selection, I'd risk getting a *B* (maybe worse) rather than an *A* on the midterm. But then I stepped back for a moment.

It was my second-to-last semester in school and probably my last chance to fully focus on and perhaps even master this subject. "I'm here to learn," I thought, so I decided to present the article and be transparent. I delivered an organized, attractive, thoughtful presentation and addressed the ideas I understood as well as the ones I didn't. I started the presentation with the following message to my professor and classmates:

This article really challenged me, and I have to be honest—some of it I understood, and some of it I didn't. But I'm presenting it today because I want to learn, and I'm hoping some of you will help me understand these principles better.

Getting those words out wasn't easy, and neither was admitting that I couldn't figure something out on my own and needed help. But would you believe my professor, a highly accomplished Ph.D. and brilliant economist, was impressed by my candor? In fact, she used my honesty as a springboard for an impromptu discussion. Instead of answering my questions outright, she asked my classmates to offer their

School isn't a place to be timid. On the contrary, it's the perfect place to take intellectual risks.

thoughts on the matter. Now, rather than feeling alone and incompetent, I felt as if we were all in it together, tackling a complex problem as a team. I received an *A* on my presentation (and in the course, believe it or not), but what's more, I confronted my fear, asked for help, and learned a lot about transparency, vulnerability, and macroeconomics in the process. The moral of this story is: School isn't a place to be timid. On the contrary, it's the perfect place to take intellectual risks.

Use your time in school to try something new, and don't be afraid to make mistakes. Education is a process of trial and error; we achieve mastery through intentional and iterated practice. Learning isn't

Learning isn't easy, but it is worth it.

easy, but it is worth it. You are blessed with the opportunity to obtain a formal education—but not everyone is. Please remember that, and don't take a moment of learning for granted.

CONCLUSION

"Nothing can stop the man with the right mental attitude from achieving his goal; nothing on earth can help the man with the wrong mental attitude."

~ THOMAS JEFFERSON

I'm so proud of you for taking the time to "sharpen the ax" by reading this book. But, more importantly, I hope you are proud of yourself for building habits that will transform your studies and your life.

If this book has been helpful to you, I encourage you to do two things:

1. First, drop me a note at Christie@get-the-degree.com and let me know which tips worked best for you. I'd love to hear from you.

2. Second, share this book with someone who can benefit from it. While I wrote it for students, many principles (eating an elephant or the rock star reading method, for instance) can be applied by anyone who wants to be more effective and efficient in their work.

Before I sign off, I want to leave you with three final hacks: totems, fight songs, and mantras. Allow me to explain.

I hesitated to put this section in the book because I thought it might be too "out there," but here's the deal: I'm not above trying anything that can help me perform better, and hopefully,

183

NOTES

you feel the same way too. So, here are some tips I've learned from trusted friends and advisors over the years.

While writing my first novel, I took a course at UCLA Extension, and my professor suggested we place a "totem," or lucky charm, at our writing stations to help facilitate the writing process. This object (which was different for everyone) was really just a signal to our brain, every time we saw it, that we were entering "writing mode."

Personally, I like to surround myself with inspirational quotes, so I usually have a couple on or near my desk. Also, as I write this, my favorite rose quartz and onyx mala beads sit perched on the base of my desk lamp because they remind me of my yoga and meditation practice and give me a sense of peace.

Speaking of yoga, I learned about "fight songs" from my favorite attorney-turned-yoga-instructor. Shout out to that special soul, Jocelyne Solomon, who once told me that on her way to the courtroom, she'd pop in her earbuds and get pumped up to win her case by listening to her favorite jam. After hearing this, I created a playlist of my own fight songs that I listened to every day on the way to work. Because transitioning from one activity or mindset to another can be challenging, having a ritual or symbol (a fight song or a totem) that signals to your brain that it's time to do something meaningful is powerful— and it works! In fact, many high performers have their own unique rituals to prepare themselves for peak performance. (Check out Tony Robbins's "priming exercise" on YouTube for his morning ritual.)

Rituals work best when you actually believe in them, and that's why mastering your mind is so important. This mastery includes positive self-talk, which is critical to your success. Even though you will meet some incredible mentors and coaches throughout your life, mentors can't be with you every second of every day. That's why you need to be your own best coach. No one knows when you need a pep talk more than you do, which is why you need to practice the art of positive self-talk, and this is where mantras come in. Truth be told, I used to think mantras and affirmations were silly until I realized I needed encouragement to succeed, and sometimes the only person available to pick me up was me.

This is the mantra I repeat whenever I feel tired, discouraged, or overwhelmed:

> *I am mighty.*
> *I am powerful.*
> *And I can do this!*

Repeat these words to yourself whenever you need a boost because you *are* mighty. You *are* powerful. And yes, you CAN do this!

I wish you all the joy and aplomb that accompanies learning. May you use your knowledge to bless and uplift others.

Sincerely,

C

ACKNOWLEDGMENTS

• • • • • • • •

First, I would like to acknowledge my grandparents. A special thanks goes to my grandfather, who bought me my first computer back when AOL was my window to the world. I'd also like to thank my strong, smart, and spirited grandmother, who sat me at an old-fashioned typewriter as a child and gave me my first typing lessons. Grandma "Cuckoo" (as I affectionately called her) taught me never to settle for anything less than perfection. Grandma and Grandpa, thank you for everything. I love you both.

I would also like to acknowledge and thank the friends and colleagues who kindly offered insights on this book: Jim Gash, Jason Jarvis, Philip Camino, Scott Cummings, Meghan Schooler, Todd McCullough, Gary Leibowitz, Brad Jenkins, and Christina Corriveau. Your unique insights made this book what it is today and pushed me to think in new and creative ways.

Thanks also goes to two of my closest friends, Kacie MacDonald and Matthew Williams. The foundation of your friendship and support makes everything I do possible. Your presence in my life is like air: seemingly invisible but undeniably indispensable. Thank you for loving me through the ups and downs and believing in me always.

Last but not least, I'd like to thank my friend and fellow author, Dr. Michael Murray, for introducing me to Morgan James Publishing. I would be remiss not to mention David Hancock and the team at MJP for their patience and helpfulness through this journey. Thank you for recognizing my vision and bringing this book to life.

ABOUT THE AUTHOR

· · · · · · · · ·

Christie is currently a higher education consultant and manager for Deloitte and has worked in higher education for more than a decade.

A former U.S. diplomat, Christie holds a master's degree in International Relations from the University of California, San Diego as well as an MBA in International Business from Pepperdine Graziadio Business School. She spent years living abroad while working as a Foreign Service Officer at the U.S. Embassy, London. When she returned to California, Christie earned a degree in Interior Design from the Fashion Institute of Design & Merchandising and served as an adjunct faculty member teaching Global Business Operations, International Relations & Negotiations, and Business Ethics.

Christie is a lifelong learner and loves sharing her knowledge through writing. Over the past twenty years, she's written for various print and online newspapers, magazines, and journals, including *The Huffington Post* and *The L.A. Times.*

She is based in Los Angeles, California, where she enjoys spending time with her friends, family, and six-pound Maltipoo. Christie loves traveling the globe as well as attending international yoga retreats. Christie is also a certified yoga and ballet barre instructor, and when she's not exercising, she can be found reading, writing, and exploring Los Angeles.

For links mentioned in this book and additional content, visit:
www.get-the-degree.com.

APPENDIX A
ADDITIONAL RESOURCES

RECOMMENDED READING

·········

Allen, David. *Getting Things Done*. London: Penguin Publishing Group, 2015.

Burnett, Bill, and Dave Evans. *Designing Your Life: How to Build a Well-Lived, Joyful Life*. New York, NY: Alfred A. Knopf, 2021.

Clear, James. *Atomic Habits: Tiny Changes, Remarkable Results: An Easy & Proven Way to Build Good Habits & Break Bad Ones*. Toronto: CELA, 2021.

Covey, Stephen R. *The 7 Habits of Highly Effective People*. New York, NY: Simon & Schuster, 2020.

Csikszentmihalyi, Mihaly. *Flow: The Psychology of Optimal Experience*. New York, NY: HarperCollins, 2008.

Dalton-Smith, Saundra. *Sacred Rest: Recover Your Life, Renew Your Energy, Restore Your Sanity*. New York, NY: Faith Words, 2019.

Fabritius, Friederike, and Hans Werner Hagemann. *The Leading Brain: Powerful Science-Based Strategies for Achieving Peak Performance*. New York, NY: Penguin Random House LLC, 2018.

Goleman, Daniel. *Focus: The Hidden Driver of Excellence*. New York, NY: HarperCollins, 2013.

Lopez, Christie Carmelle. "Matcha, Get It While It's Hot! A 2016 Lifestyle Trend." HuffPost Blog. HuffPost, February 8, 2016. https://www.huffpost.com/entry/get-it-while-its-hot-matc_b_9117056.

Miller, Dan. *48 Days to the Work and Life You Love: Find It—or Create It*. New York, NY: Morgan James Publishing, 2020.

Newport, Cal. *Deep Work: Rules for Focused Success in a Distracted World*. New York, NY: Grand Central Publishing, 2016.

Rath, Tom. *Strengths Finder 2.0*. New York, NY: Gallup Press, 2007.

Sinek, Simon. *Start with Why: How Great Leaders Inspire Everyone to Take Action*. London: Penguin Books Ltd, 2011.

WRITING RESOURCES

·········

Must-Have Resources

The Elements of Style by William Strunk and E.B. White

The Chicago Manual of Style [most recent edition], University of Chicago Press

A Manual for Writers of Research Papers, Theses, and Dissertations, Ninth Edition: Chicago Style for Students and Researchers by Kate L. Turabian

Cite Right, Third Edition: A Quick Guide to Citation Styles—MLA, APA, Chicago, the Sciences, Professions, and More by Charles Lipson

Online Tools and Applications

Grammarly

Hemingway Editor

Purdue Online Writing Lab Citation Resources & Citation Generator

For Further Reading

100 Ways to Improve Your Writing: Proven Professional Techniques for Writing with Style and Power by Gary Provost

Eats, Shoots & Leaves: The Zero Tolerance Approach to Punctuation by Lynne Truss

On Writing Well: The Classic Guide to Writing Nonfiction by William Zinsser

Writing Tools: 55 Essential Strategies for Every Writer by Roy Peter Clark

APPENDIX B
TABLES AND FIGURES

Figure 1: Bloom's Taxonomy

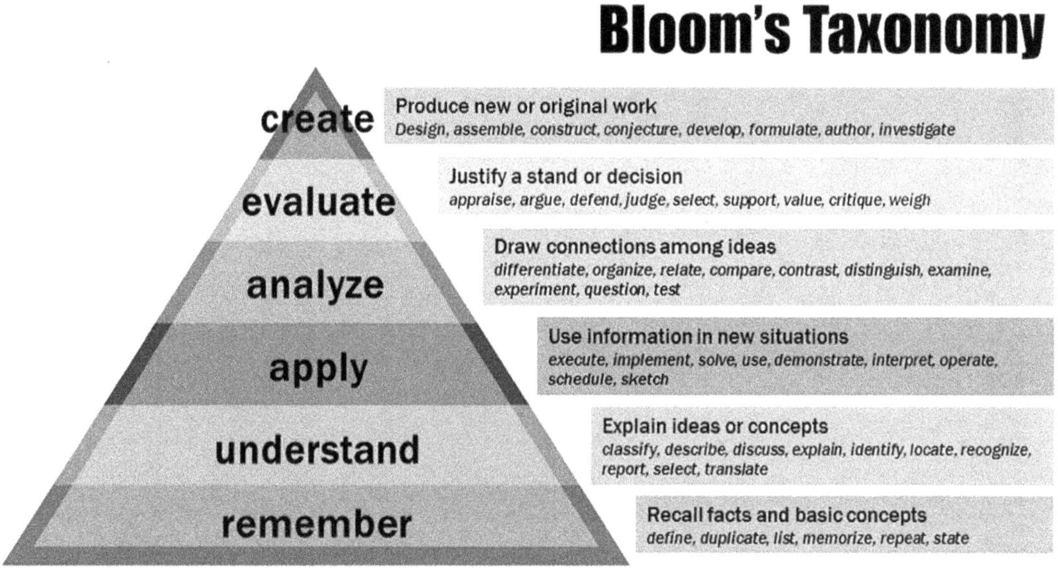

Reproduced with permission. Source: Armstrong, P. (2010). Bloom's Taxonomy. Vanderbilt University Center for Teaching. Retrieved June 21, 2022, from https://cft.vanderbilt.edu/guides-sub-pages/blooms-taxonomy/.

Figure 2: Time Management Worksheet

Time Management Sheet

Time	Monday	Tuesday	Wednesday	Thursday	Friday	Saturday	Sunday
5:00							
5:30							
6:00							
6:30							
7:00							
7:30							
8:00							
8:30							
9:00							
9:30							
10:00							
10:30							
11:00							
11:30							
12:00							
12:30							
1:00							
1:30							
2:00							
2:30							
3:00							
3:30							
4:00							
4:30							
5:00							
5:30							
6:00							
6:30							
7:00							
7:30							
8:00							
8:30							
9:00							
9:30							
10:00							
10:30							
11:00							
11:30							

Figure 3: SMART Goals Matrix

Specific	Measurable	Achievable	Relevant	Time-bound
Well-defined, clear, and unambiguous goals.	Goal includes specific criteria to measure progress toward and achievement of the goal.	A goal that is attainable; not impossible to achieve given the existing timeframe or resources.	A goal that relates to and supports a broader purpose (either personally or within an organization).	A goal with a clearly defined timeline, including a start date and a target date.
What will be accomplished? What actions will you take?	*What quantitative data will you use to measure the goal? (Think in numbers.) This can be a financial sum, quantity, percentage, or deadline.*	*Is the goal doable? Do you have the necessary skills and resources?*	*How does the goal align with broader objectives? Why is the result important?*	*What is the time frame for accomplishing the goal? Does the deadline create urgency, while also remaining achievable?*

Project Planning Worksheet

| Project Title: |
| Deadline: |
| Tasks: |

Project Timeline

Due Date	Task / Subtask
	Final Deadline - Project Complete

Project Planning Worksheet

Project Title:	
Deadline:	
Tasks:	

Project Timeline	
Due Date	**Task / Subtask**
	Final Deadline - Project Complete

Questions, Key Terms, Main Ideas	Notes

Summary

Questions, Key Terms, Main Ideas	Notes

Summary

Questions, Key Terms, Main Ideas	Notes

Summary

Questions, Key Terms, Main Ideas	Notes

Summary

ENDNOTES

· · · · · · · · ·

Chapter 1: Know Your Why

1   Stephen R. Covey, The 7 Habits of Highly Effective People (New York, NY: Simon & Schuster, 2020), 111.

2   For more, read Simon Sinek's *Start with Why: How Great Leaders Inspire Everyone to Take Action.*

3   Stephen R. Covey, *The 7 Habits of Highly Effective People* (New York, NY: Simon & Schuster, 2020), 173.

4   Laura Vanderkam, *What the Most Successful People Do Before Breakfast: How to Achieve More at Work and at Home* (New York, NY: Penguin, 2013), 11.

5   Cell Press. "Evidence That Human Brains Replay Our Waking Experiences While We Sleep." ScienceDaily, May 5, 2020. https://www.sciencedaily.com/releases/2020/05/200505121711.htm.

6   Daniel H. Pink, *When the Scientific Secrets of Perfect Timing* (New York, NY: Riverhead Books, 2019), 26-35.

Chapter 3: Timeout!

7   James Clear, *Atomic Habits: An Easy & Proven Way to Build Good Habits & Break Bad Ones* (New York, NY: Penguin Random House, 2018), 70–75.

Chapter 5: Read Like a Rock Star

8   Drucker, Peter. "Managing Oneself." Harvard Business Review. Harvard Business Review, October 19, 2022. https://hbr.org/2005/01/managing-oneself.

Chapter 6: Making Minutes Matter

9   Daniel Goleman, *Focus: The Hidden Driver of Excellence* (New York, NY: HarperCollins, 2013), 16.

10 For more on flow, read the work of Mihaly Csikszentmihalyi.

11 Amrita Mandal, "The Pomodoro Technique: An Effective Time Management Tool," Eunice Kennedy Shriver National Institute of Child Health and Human Development (U.S. Department of Health and Human Services, May 2020), https://science.nichd.nih.gov/confluence/display/newsletter/2020/05/07/The+Pomodoro+Technique%3A+An+Effective+Time+Management+Tool.

12 Evans, Lisa. "The Exact Amount of Time You Should Work Every Day." Fast Company, September 15, 2014. https://www.fastcompany.com/3035605/the-exact-amount-of-time-you-should-work-every-day.

Chapter 7: Before You Begin

13 "Seven Standards of Quality Journalism," News Literacy Project, January 24, 2022, https://newslit.org/educators/resources/seven-standards-quality-journalism/.

14 "SPJ Code of Ethics," Society of Professional Journalists, accessed October 10, 2022, https://www.spj.org/ethicscode.asp.

Chapter 8: Prewriting

15 https://www.youtube.com/watch?v=Rvey9g0VgY0

16 Oppenheimer, Daniel M. 2006. "Consequences of Erudite Vernacular Utilized Irrespective of Necessity: Problems with Using Long Words Needlessly." *Applied Cognitive Psychology* 20 (2): 139–56. doi:10.1002/acp.1178.

Chapter 9: Writing: A Process-Driven Approach

17 https://owl.purdue.edu/owl/research_and_citation/resources.htmlhere.

Chapter 11: Everything Else

18 Allen, David. *Getting Things Done.* London: Penguin Publishing Group, 2015.

Chapter 12: Biohacking for Scholars

19 Janna Mantua and Guido Simonelli, "Sleep Duration and Cognition: Is There an Ideal Amount?," Sleep (Oxford University Press, January 12, 2019), https://academic.oup.com/sleep/article/42/3/zsz010/5288680.

20 Max Hirshkowitz et al., "National Sleep Foundation's Updated Sleep Duration Recommendations: Final Report," Sleep Health (Science Direct, October 31, 2015), https://www.sciencedirect.com/science/article/abs/pii/S2352721815001606.

21 Sanjay Gupta, *12 Weeks to a Sharper You: A Guided Program* (New York, NY: Simon & Schuster, 2022), 24.

22 Patricia C García-Suárez et al., "Acute Systemic Response of BDNF, Lactate and Cortisol to Strenuous Exercise Modalities in Healthy Untrained Women," Dose-response: a publication of International Hormesis Society (U.S. National Library of Medicine, December 10, 2020), https://www.ncbi.nlm.nih.gov/pmc/articles/PMC7734519/.

23 Huberman, Andrew. "Huberman Lab Neural Network," January 24, 2023.

24 Huberman, Andrew. "Huberman Lab Neural Network," January 24, 2023.

25 Andrew Huberman, Huberman Lab, podcast audio, September 5, 2022, https://podcasts.apple.com/us/podcast/huberman-lab/id1545953110?i=1000578389076.

26 Christie Carmelle Lopez, "Matcha, Get It While It's Hot! A 2016 Lifestyle Trend," The Blog (HuffPost, December 7, 2017), https://www.huffpost.com/entry/get-it-while-its-hot-matc_b_9117056.

27 Kris Gunnars, "10 Proven Health Benefits of Turmeric and Curcumin," Healthline (Healthline Media, May 7, 2021), https://www.healthline.com/nutrition/top-10-evidence-based-health-benefits-of-turmeric#TOC_TITLE_HDR_8.

28 S.R. Venkat, "Lion's Mane Mushrooms: What Are the Benefits," Nourish (WebMD, May 20, 2022), https://www.webmd.com/diet/what-are-the-health-benefits-of-lions-mane-mushrooms.

29 "Reishi Mushrooms: Health Benefits, Safety Information, Dosage, and More," Nourish (WebMD, November 23, 2022), https://www.webmd.com/diet/health-benefits-reishi-mushrooms.

30 Asprey, Dave. "How to Make Your Coffee Bulletproof and Your Morning Too." Dave Asprey, September 28, 2021. https://daveasprey.com/how-to-make-your-coffee-bulletproof-and-your-morning-too/.

31 Giannos, P., Prokopidis, K., Lidoriki, I. et al. "Medium-chain Triglycerides May Improve Memory in Non-demented Older Adults: A Systematic Review of Randomized Controlled Trials," BMC Geriatr 22, 817 (2022), https://doi.org/10.1186/s12877-022-03521-6

32 Jourdan Arnaud, "What Are Binaural Beats and How Can They Help You Focus?" The Los Angeles Film School, September 15, 2022, https://www.lafilm.edu/blog/what-are-binaural-beats-and-how-can-they-help-you-focus/.

33 Jacquelyn Cafasso, "Binaural Beats: Sleep, Therapy, and Meditation," Healthline (Healthline Media, September 18, 2018), https://www.healthline.com/health/binaural-beats#instructions.

34 James J DiNicolantonio and James H O'Keefe, "The Importance of Marine Omega-3s for Brain Development and the Prevention and Treatment of Behavior, Mood, and Other Brain Disorders," U.S. National Library of Medicine (Nutrients, August 4, 2020), https://www.ncbi.nlm.nih.gov/pmc/articles/PMC7468918/.

35 Chia-Yu Chang, Der-Shin Ke, and Jen-Yin Chen, "Essential Fatty Acids and Human Brain," U.S. National Library of Medicine (Acta Neurol Taiwan, December 2009), https://pubmed.ncbi.nlm.nih.gov/20329590/#:~:text=The%20human%20brain%20is%20nearly,integrity%20and%20ability%20to%20perform.

36 "Omega-3 Fatty Acids: An Essential Contribution," The Nutrition Source (Harvard School of Public Health, May 22, 2019), https://www.hsph.harvard.edu/nutritionsource/what-should-you-eat/fats-and-cholesterol/types-of-fat/omega-3-fats/#:~:text=Likely%20due%20to%20these%20effects,key%20family%20of%20polyunsaturated%20fats.

37 Andrew Huberman, Huberman Lab, podcast audio, September 5, 2022, https://podcasts.apple.com/us/podcast/huberman-lab/id1545953110?i=1000578389076.

38 Colleen DeBoer, "Best Foods for a Healthy Brain," Healthbeat (Northwestern Medicine), accessed January 8, 2023, https://www.nm.org/healthbeat/healthy-

tips/nutrition/best-food-for-a-healthy-brain#:~:text=Nuts%20like%20
almonds%2C%20pistachios%20and,certainly%20goes%20to%20the%20
walnut.

39 Robert H. Shmerling, "Your Brain on Chocolate," Harvard Health (Harvard Health Publishing, Harvard Medical School, August 16, 2017), https://www.health.harvard.edu/blog/your-brain-on-chocolate-2017081612179.

40 Gunnars, Kris. "6 Reasons Why Eggs Are the Healthiest Food on the Planet." Healthline. Healthline Media, April 26, 2018. https://www.healthline.com/nutrition/6-reasons-why-eggs-are-the-healthiest-food-on-the-planet#TOC_TITLE_HDR_6.

41 Ensle, Karen. "Eat Berries to Improve Brain Function." Eat Berries to Improve Brain Function (Rutgers NJAES), June 2017. https://njaes.rutgers.edu/sshw/message/message.php?p=Health&m=350#:~:text=Below%20are%20some%20reasons%20to,and%20attention%20to%20required%20tasks.

42 Colleen DeBoer, "Best Foods for a Healthy Brain," Healthbeat (Northwestern Medicine), accessed January 8, 2023, https://www.nm.org/healthbeat/healthy-tips/nutrition/best-food-for-a-healthy-brain#:~:text=Nuts%20like%20almonds%2C%20pistachios%20and,certainly%20goes%20to%20the%20walnut

43 Kerri-Ann Jennings, "11 Best Foods to Boost Your Brain and Memory," Healthline (Healthline Media, June 18, 2021), https://www.healthline.com/nutrition/11-brain-foods#TOC_TITLE_HDR_10.

44 Colleen DeBoer, "Best Foods for a Healthy Brain," Healthbeat (Northwestern Medicine), accessed January 8, 2023, https://www.nm.org/healthbeat/healthy-tips/nutrition/best-food-for-a-healthy-brain#:~:text=Nuts%20like%20almonds%2C%20pistachios%20and,certainly%20goes%20to%20the%20walnut

45 Kerri-Ann Jennings, "11 Best Foods to Boost Your Brain and Memory," Healthline (Healthline Media, June 18, 2021), https://www.healthline.com/nutrition/11-brain-foods#TOC_TITLE_HDR_10.

46 Andrew Huberman, Huberman Lab, podcast audio, September 5, 2022, https://podcasts.apple.com/us/podcast/huberman-lab/id1545953110?i=1000578389076.

47 "What Meditation Can Do for Your Mind, Mood, and Health," Harvard Health (Harvard Health Publishing, Harvard Medical School, July 16, 2014), https://www.health.harvard.edu/staying-healthy/what-meditation-can-do-for-your-mind-mood-and-health-.

48 Brown, Joshua, and Joel Wong. "How Gratitude Changes You and Your Brain." Greater Good. The Greater Good Science Center at the University of California, Berkeley, June 6, 2017. https://greatergood.berkeley.edu/article/item/how_gratitude_changes_you_and_your_brain.

49 "Dopamine: What It Is, Function & Symptoms," Cleveland Clinic, accessed January 8, 2023, https://my.clevelandclinic.org/health/articles/22581-dopamine.

50 Andrew Huberman, interview by Lewis Howes, "1016 The Science of a Success Mindset with Neuroscientist Andrew Huberman." *The School of Greatness,* October 7, 2020.

51 Andrew Huberman, Huberman Lab, podcast audio, September 5, 2022, https://podcasts.apple.com/us/podcast/huberman-lab/id1545953110?i=1000578389076.

52 Anwar, Yasmin. "An Afternoon Nap Markedly Boosts the Brain's Learning Capacity." Berkeley News, February 22, 2010. https://news.berkeley.edu/2010/02/22/naps_boost_learning_capacity.

53 Daniel H. Pink, *When: The Scientific Secrets of Perfect Timing* (New York, NY: Riverhead Books, 2019).

54 "What Is Yoga Nidra?" Cleveland Clinic (Cleveland Clinic, September 14, 2020), https://health.clevelandclinic.org/what-is-yoga-nidra/.

Chapter 13: Career Development

55 Dizikes, Peter. "The Power of Weak Ties in Gaining New Employment." MIT News. Massachusetts Institute of Technology, September 15, 2022. https://news.mit.edu/2022/weak-ties-linkedin-employment-0915.

56 Miller, Dan. *48 Days to The Work You Love.* Nashville, TN: B & H Publishing Group, 2015.

57 Helgesen, Sally, and Marshall Goldsmith. *How Women Rise.* New York, NY: Hachette, 2018.

58 Allas, Tera, and Bill Schaninger. "The Boss Factor: Making the World a Better Place through Workplace Relationships." McKinsey & Company. McKinsey & Company, March 14, 2022. https://www.mckinsey.com/capabilities/people-and-organizational-performance/our-insights/the-boss-factor-making-the-world-a-better-place-through-workplace-relationships.

59 "Why People Quit Their Jobs." Harvard Business Review, August 23, 2016. https://hbr.org/2016/09/why-people-quit-their-jobs#:~:text=Some%20of%20this%20analytical%20work,have%20held%20steady%20for%20years.

60 Patel, Alok, and Stephanie Plowman. "The Increasing Importance of a Best Friend at Work." Gallup.com. Gallup, November 10, 2022. https://www.gallup.com/workplace/397058/increasing-importance-best-friend-work.aspx.

61 Csikszentmihalyi, Mihaly. Creativity. New York, NY: HarperCollins, 1996.

Chapter 14: The Last Lesson

62 Hougaard, Rasmus, and Jacqueline Carter. "If You Aspire to Be a Great Leader, Be Present." Harvard Business Review. Harvard Business Review, November 27, 2019. https://hbr.org/2017/12/if-you-aspire-to-be-a-great-leader-be-present.

63 Hougaard, Rasmus, and Jacqueline Carter. "If You Aspire to Be a Great Leader, Be Present." Harvard Business Review. Harvard Business Review, November 27, 2019. https://hbr.org/2017/12/if-you-aspire-to-be-a-great-leader-be-present.

64 Cell Press. "Evidence That Human Brains Replay Our Waking Experiences While We Sleep." ScienceDaily, May 5, 2020. https://www.sciencedaily.com/releases/2020/05/200505121711.htm.

65 Daniel Goleman, *Focus: The Hidden Driver of Excellence* (New York, NY: HarperCollins, 2013), 56.

66 Dalton-Smith, Saundra. *Sacred Rest: Recover Your Life, Renew Your Energy, Restore Your Sanity.* New York, NY: Faith Words, 2019.

67 Studies show a parabolic relationship between sleep and cognitive function with seven hours of sleep each night being optimal. Mantua, Janna, and Guido Simonelli. "Sleep Duration and Cognition: Is There an Ideal Amount?" Sleep 42, no. 3 (March 2019). https://doi.org/10.1093/sleep/zsz010.

68 Arnsten, Amy, Carolyn M. Mazure, and Rajita Sinha. "Everyday Stress Can Shut down the Brain's Chief Command Center." Scientific American. Scientific American, April 1, 2012. https://www.scientificamerican.com/article/this-is-your-brain-in-meltdown/.

69 Walton, Alice G. "7 Ways Meditation Can Actually Change the Brain." Forbes. Forbes Magazine, April 14, 2022. https://www.forbes.com/sites/alicegwalton/2015/02/09/7-ways-meditation-can-actually-change-the-brain/?sh=1f3d8c951465.

70 Luke 17:11–19

71 Daniel Goleman, *Focus: The Hidden Driver of Excellence* (New York, NY: HarperCollins, 2013), 170.

72 Davidson, Katey. "11 Natural Ways to Lower Your Cortisol Levels." Healthline. Healthline Media, June 11, 2021. https://www.healthline.com/nutrition/ways-to-lower-cortisol#TOC_TITLE_HDR_5.

73 Davidson, Katey. "11 Natural Ways to Lower Your Cortisol Levels." Healthline. Healthline Media, June 11, 2021. https://www.healthline.com/nutrition/ways-to-lower-cortisol#TOC_TITLE_HDR_5.

74 Andrew Huberman, interview by Matt Abrahams, "Best of: Lessons from Neuroscientist Andrew Huberman." *Thank Fast, Talk Smart*, August 30, 2022.

75 Vlemincx, Elke, Ilse Van Diest, and Omer Van den Bergh. "A Sigh Following Sustained Attention and Mental Stress: Effects on Respiratory Variability." Physiology & Behavior. Elsevier, May 23, 2012. https://www.sciencedirect.com/science/article/abs/pii/S0031938412002004?via%3Dihub.

76 Andrew Huberman, interview by Matt Abrahams, "Best of: Lessons from Neuroscientist Andrew Huberman." *Thank Fast, Talk Smart*, August 30, 2022.

"Take the first step in faith. You don't have to see the whole staircase, just take the first step."

~ *Martin Luther King Jr.*

Printed in the USA
CPSIA information can be obtained
at www.ICGtesting.com
JSHW051743190424
61528JS00004B/7